Stripples
STRIKES AGAIN!

More Quilts to Make with
the Bias Stripper™ Ruler

Donna Lynn Thomas

Dedication

This book is dedicated to the sweet things in life; my friends and family in all their extensions and facets, but foremost to my husband, Terry, my sons, Joseph and Peter, and my loyal shadow, Miss Maggie. I wish all were so blessed.

Acknowledgments

There are always so many people to thank when it comes time to finish a book. Many contribute their talents, thoughts, and insights to the process.

A big thank you goes to Nancy J. Martin for introducing me to my first bias square in June 1987. She set my little gray cells churning and burning!

Many, many thanks go to the pattern testers, quiltmakers, and quilters who give life, substance, and color to the book; Gabriel Pursell, Dee Glenn, Floy Heidenreich, Sally Schneider, Beth Rhodes, Kari Lane, Robin Chambers, Ursula Reikes, Mildred Gerdes, Deb Rose, Linda Kittle, Beth Wagenaar, Norma Jean Rohman, Aline Duerr, Charlotte Freeman, Betty Gilliam, Ann Woodward, and Judy Keller. Thank you all, your talents are priceless!

A special thanks to Judi Rutherford for proofreading and listening and providing much-needed third-party assessment.

Marion Shelton has the warmest voice, softest shoulder, and biggest heart. She's always there for her authors. From the bottom of my heart, Marion; thanks.

Thanks and much more to Ursula Reikes, my technical editor and friend. It's always a delight to talk and laugh and work with her. I am so spoiled!

CREDITS

EDITOR-IN-CHIEF	KERRY I. SMITH
TECHNICAL EDITOR	URSULA REIKES
MANAGING EDITOR	JUDY PETRY
COPY EDITOR	TINA COOK
PROOFREADER	LESLIE PHILLIPS
DESIGN DIRECTOR	CHERYL STEVENSON
TEXT DESIGNER	KAY GREEN
COVER DESIGNER	JOANNE LAUTERJUNG
PRODUCTION ASSISTANT	MARIJANE FIGG
ILLUSTRATOR	ROBIN STROBEL
PHOTOGRAPHER	BRENT KANE

Stripples Strikes Again!
More Quilts to Make with the Bias Stripper™ Ruler
©1997 by Donna Lynn Thomas

That Patchwork Place, Inc., PO Box 118
Bothell, WA 98041-0118 USA

Printed in Hong Kong
02 01 00 99 98 97   6 5 4 3 2 1

Library of Congress Cataloging-in-Publication Data

Thomas, Donna Lynn
  Stripples strikes again! : more quilts to make with the bias stripper ruler / Donna Lynn Thomas.
    p. cm.
  ISBN 1-56477-195-4
  1. Patchwork—Patterns. 2. Rotary cutting. 3. Quilting—Patterns.
  I. Title.
TT835.T4635 1997
746.46'041—dc21

97-15932
CIP

MISSION STATEMENT

WE ARE DEDICATED TO PROVIDING QUALITY PRODUCTS AND SERVICE BY WORKING TOGETHER TO INSPIRE CREATIVITY AND TO ENRICH THE LIVES WE TOUCH.

TABLE OF CONTENTS

INTRODUCTION

Just what is bias strip piecing? It is similar in many ways to straight-grain strip piecing, for which you cut strips from selvage to selvage along the straight grain, sew the strips into units, and then cut the units into segments. The presewn and prepressed segments take the place of individually cut and sewn squares, triangles, and rectangles in patchwork. Increased speed and accuracy are two benefits of the process.

With bias strip piecing you cut strips along the bias grain instead of on the straight grain, sew the bias strips into units, and then cut the units into shapes for piecing. Use bias strip piecing any time you want the edge of the unit on the straight grain and any interior seams on the bias. Many common patchwork units lend themselves to bias strip piecing.

The goal of *Stripples Strikes Again!* is to present a comprehensive guide to bias strip piecing and to share the many uses of the Bias Stripper™ ruler. Bias strip piecing was first used to make simple bias squares, that is, two right triangles joined on their long bias edges. You can use standard rotary rulers when cutting bias strips for simple units such as bias squares, but these methods involve conversion charts or messy math and a lot of wasted fabric. In addition, you can't measure the width of diagonal bias strips with a standard ruler. This isn't much of a problem with simple units that can be trimmed to size, but as soon as you begin to make units with interior strips, the need for accurate strip widths becomes apparent. For example, the center strip in a Nine Patch strip unit must be a precise width. Theoretically, the two outside strips in a Nine Patch strip unit could be oversized and cut back to size later, but not the center strip; its finished size is determined as soon as it is sewn into the strip unit. The same is true for the center strips in bias strip-pieced units.

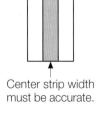

Center strip width must be accurate.

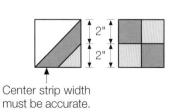

Center strip width must be accurate.

So how is the Bias Stripper different from a regular rotary ruler? The Bias Stripper measures differently than a standard ruler does. Traditional rotary rulers measure the width of a strip. This is what you want when you're making units that must measure evenly from side to side, such as plain squares.

When you move into bias strip piecing, things change a little. You want the bias strip to measure evenly where it falls *on the edge* of the cut unit so that it will fit with other squares and triangles in the block. The diagonal of the bias strip is the measurement that falls on the edge of the unit. Unlike standard rotary rulers, which measure side-to-side dimensions on strips, the Bias Stripper is *designed to measure and cut strips that have even diagonal measurements.*

An added benefit of the Bias Stripper is that it makes it simple to figure accurate strip widths for simple bias units, such as bias squares, without charts or fancy math. The ½" margin on the edge of the ruler provides for the two seam allowances on either side of the strip.

Since the Bias Stripper measures diagonal strip widths, it is also the perfect tool to cut plain squares and bias squares that measure evenly across the diagonal. These units are desirable for on-point piecing situations such as those found in many blocks and borders. In the past, without the Bias Stripper, you had to struggle with templates or inadequate methods to deal with these situations. Now with the Bias Stripper, you can use rotary cutting and strip piecing methods to painlessly produce these on-point units with precision.

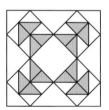

Bias squares in block need to measure evenly across the diagonal.

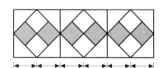

Squares in pieced border need to measure evenly on the diagonal to fit a quilt.

As you read and work through *Stripples Strikes Again!* you will see the tremendous potential for bias strip piecing and on-point construction in your own quilt designs. With the guidelines provided for designing bias strip units, you will be able to apply the techniques to your own quilts, not just to those in this book.

EQUIPMENT AND SUPPLIES

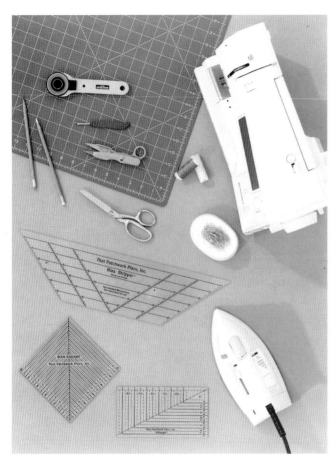

SEWING MACHINE. You need a sewing machine in good working order. Use a size 70/10 or 80/12 needle and replace it with each new quilt or when you hear a popping noise every time the needle pierces the fabric. Set your machine to about 12 stitches per inch or to the standard setting suggested for your machine.

THREAD. Use high quality, 100% cotton thread. Cotton-covered polyester is an adequate substitute. If most of the fabrics in my quilt are dark, I use a dark gray thread, and if most of the fabrics are light, I use a cream or very light gray thread.

MISCELLANEOUS SEWING SUPPLIES. General sewing items, such as fabric shears, silk pins, thread clips, seam ripper, sewing needles, quilting needles, and quilting thread, should be part of your basic quilt-making kit.

IRONING EQUIPMENT. Ironing tools don't need to be fancy, just clean and operable. Use a traditional ironing board or a terry cloth towel on a heat-resistant surface. Set your iron for cotton. Keep ironing equipment near your sewing machine; you'll need to press frequently. Keep a plastic spray bottle filled with water handy.

ROTARY CUTTER AND MAT. There are many brands and styles of rotary cutters available. The larger cutters are better for cutting through several layers of fabric. Rotary cutters have extremely sharp blades. Handle them with care and respect. Never leave the blade exposed, even for a minute.

You need a specially designed rotary mat to use with your rotary cutter. If you try to cut on any other surface, you will ruin not only the cutting surface but also the cutting blade. An 18" x 24" mat is the smallest you should have for general quiltmaking. Store mats flat and avoid extreme hot or cold temperatures, which can cause warping.

GENERAL-PURPOSE ROTARY RULER. A good rotary ruler is an invaluable tool and an absolute necessity for rotary cutting. Look for a ruler made of 1/8" thick acrylic that has an allover 1" grid and 1/8" markings on the grid lines. The 1/8" markings are important because many rotary-cut quilt patterns use 1/8" increments.

At the minimum, you should have a 6" x 12" ruler to perform most general cutting. If you can afford it, a larger ruler, such as 6" x 24", is useful also. A 15" square ruler can be handy for cutting oversized pieces.

THE BIAS STRIPPER RULER. Use this ruler only for the special techniques described in this book. Do not use it for general-purpose cutting—it has non-standard measurements. It is a necessary tool for making the quilts in this book. See pages 13–26 to learn how to use it.

THE BIAS SQUARE® RULER. This is a square cutting guide designed exclusively for cutting bias squares from bias strip units. In addition to its intended use, it performs many other rotary-cutting functions.

THE BIRANGLE™ RULER. This ruler is useful for cutting striped rectangles from bias strip units. Although you don't need a BiRangle to cut striped rectangles, the markings make it easy to see the rectangles you are cutting.

FABRIC

Selecting Fabric

I base my fabric selections on color palettes, and the palette I use depends on the look I want for the finished quilt. A *fixed palette* describes a limited number of fabrics, each assigned to a specific place in the quilt pattern. To assemble a fixed palette, choose one "anchor" print, such as a multicolor floral or paisley. You can feature it prominently in the quilt block or you can use it in the border. In either case, coordinate all your other fabrics with this main print. Keep the palette interesting by choosing fabrics in a variety of scales and pattern styles. "Desert Dogs" on page 30 is a good example of a fixed palette. The border print was the anchor for this quilt.

Scrappy or multi-fabric quilts are my favorites. There are several ways to select fabrics for a scrappy quilt. A *color-family scrap quilt* is one in which a color family is assigned to a particular place in the quilt or quilt block. Then, a variety of prints within that color family are chosen and used randomly in the assigned position. "Starweave" on page 31 is an example of a color-family scrap quilt.

Another way to make a scrappy quilt is to assign dark and light values to specific positions in the quilt or block. Choose a variety of prints and colors in the appropriate value for each assigned position.

I frequently combine elements of different approaches. I might make a pair of blocks based on a certain color or value combination, and then make additional pairs based on the same combination but use different fabrics each time. You can choose all manner of glorious colors to make a rich quilt in a simple way. "Bob's Lost Ships" on page 28 is a good example of a color-family two-block approach, and "Next Door Neighbor" on page 33 is an example of scrappy two-block approach.

Preparing Fabric

Before prewashing your fabrics, it's a good idea to check them for bleeding. Soak dark and light fabrics separately in warm water. If the water is clear after twenty minutes, the fabric is ready for prewashing. If not, rinse and soak again. If the fabric still bleeds after several rinses with no sign of letting up, do not use the fabric.

Once fabrics pass the bleeding test, wash them in warm water with sudsy ammonia (¼ cup for a machine or 1 tablespoon for a sink) or with commercial quilt soap. Do not use laundry detergent because it can fade fabrics or cause otherwise stable dyes to bleed. Dry on low to medium heat until damp dry. Press with a hot iron. Gently straighten and refold your fabric, selvage to selvage, as it was when you bought it.

Understanding Fabric and Grain Line

Fabric from the bolt has two finished edges, called *selvages*. The lengthwise grain of fabric runs parallel to the selvages and has little or no give. The crosswise grain of fabric runs from selvage to selvage and has a slight amount of give. Both crosswise and lengthwise grains are called *straight grain* because they run parallel to the woven yarns in the fabric. The *true bias* runs at a 45° angle to the lengthwise and crosswise grains and has a generous amount of give.

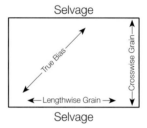

Many fabrics stretch off grain as they are rolled onto bolts. You can sometimes straighten a piece of fabric that is badly off grain by gently pulling opposite corners.

Cut all strips, squares, and rectangles on the straight grain. The edges of some shapes, such as triangles, can not all be on grain. Therefore, it is a good idea to look at the position of the piece in the pattern and consider these guidelines when deciding which edges to cut on grain.

Rule 1: Keep all perimeter edges of a quilt block on the straight grain so that the block will not stretch out of shape.

Rule 2: Whenever possible without violating Rule 1, sew a bias edge to a straight-grain edge to stabilize the seam.

BASIC ROTARY CUTTING

Creating an Even Cutting Edge

Most rotary cutting involves cutting strips of fabric and then crosscutting the strips or sewing them into units. To cut accurate strips, you need to create an even cutting edge.

1. Lay freshly pressed fabric on the rotary mat with the fold toward you and the selvages aligned at the top of the mat. If you are using a 12"-long ruler, fold the fabric again to bring the fold at the bottom up to the selvage edges at the top.

2. Place your rotary ruler just inside the raw edges of all the fabric layers at the left-hand edge. (If you are left-handed, cut from the right edge of your fabric and reverse the directions given here.) Place the edge of a Bias Square ruler on the bottom fold of the fabric and adjust the rotary ruler so that it is flush with the Bias Square. Aligning the Bias Square with the fold ensures a clean cut that is at right angles to the bottom fold and eliminates bent or V-shaped strips.

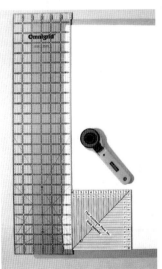

3. Hold the rotary ruler securely in place. Anchor it by placing your fingers or the palm of your hand on the mat, to the side of the ruler. Move the Bias Square aside. Cut away from yourself with firm, downward pressure, rolling the blade along the ruler's edge. Make one clean, firm cut, starting below the fold and continuing through the selvages. You may need to "walk" your hand up the ruler as you cut to keep it from shifting. If the blade is not cutting through all the layers, exert a stronger downward pressure or check the blade for nicks or dullness. Sometimes a seemingly dull blade simply needs cleaning with a lint-free cloth and a drop of sewing-machine oil behind the guard.

Cutting Strips

Once you have a clean-cut edge, you can cut strips accurately. Align the desired width measurement on the ruler with the clean edge of the fabric. If you are right-handed, the cutting edge will be on the left and you will cut strips from left to right across the fabric. If you are left-handed, the cutting edge will be on the right and you will cut strips from right to left across the fabric. In the photo, the ruler is aligned for a right-handed person to cut a 2½"-wide strip.

To prevent a bent strip, always place one of the ruler's horizontal lines on the bottom fold of the fabric. Cut the strip from bottom to top, away from yourself, as you did when cutting the clean edge.

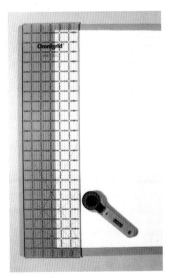

In rotary cutting, the ¼"-wide seam allowances are included in all cut dimensions. Therefore, strips for straight-grain strip piecing, squares, bars, and rectangles are always cut ½" wider than the finished measurements of the desired unit.

Cutting Squares

Squares are cut ½" larger than the desired finished size. Cut strips the width of the square's cut size. Turn the strips and cut squares from the strips crosswise. Be sure to align one of the ruler's horizontal lines across the bottom of the strip before each cut.

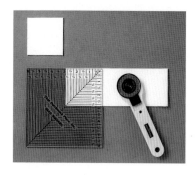

Cutting Rectangles

Rectangles are cut ½" larger than the desired finished width and height. Cut strips the width of the rectangle's cut width. Turn the strip and cut units the cut length of the rectangle.

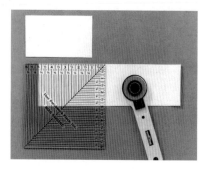

Cutting Half-Square Triangles

Make half-square triangles by cutting a square once diagonally, so the straight grain is on the two short edges. When these triangles are used in a block, the short edges fall at the outside edges of the block.

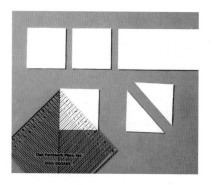

To determine the size of the square that will yield 2 half-square triangles, including seam allowances, add ⅞" to the desired finished size of the short edge of the triangle. Cut a square this size and then cut it once diagonally to yield 2 triangles.

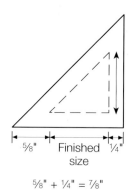

⅝" + ¼" = ⅞"

Nubbing triangle points removes excess fabric that extends beyond the ¼"-wide seam allowances, making the edges of squares and triangles easier to match for more accurate stitching. Even with triangles, nubbing eliminates the need to go back and trim the "dog ears" that remain after you sew a seam.

To nub half-square triangles, add ½" to the finished size of the triangle's short side. For example, add ½" to a 1½" finished-size triangle to get 2". Place a Bias Square ruler on the corner of the triangle at the 2" mark as shown. Cut off tips that extend beyond the ruler's edges.

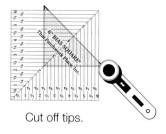

Cut off tips.

Cutting Quarter-Square Triangles

Make quarter-square triangles by cutting a square twice diagonally; the straight grain is on the long edge of each triangle. When these triangles are positioned in a block, the long edges are along the outer edges of the block.

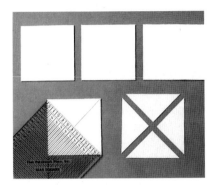

To determine the size of the square to cut, including seam allowances, add $1\frac{1}{4}$" to the desired finished size of the long edge of the triangle. Cut a square this size and then cut it twice diagonally to yield 4 triangles.

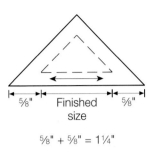

$\frac{5}{8}$" Finished size

$\frac{5}{8}$" + $\frac{5}{8}$" = $1\frac{1}{4}$"

Cutting Triangles for Diagonally Set Quilts

Cut sizes for squares that will yield side and corner setting triangles are provided in the directions for each quilt. But it's a good idea to know how to calculate the square size in case you want to change the dimensions of a quilt.

Use quarter-square triangles for side triangles at the outer edges of diagonally set quilts. When setting quilt blocks together diagonally, it's wise to cut the setting triangles slightly oversized and then trim the edges of the quilt top later. To cut quarter-square triangles, you need to know the finished size of the triangle's long edge. To determine a slightly oversized measurement, multiply the quilt block size by 1.5, and then add $1\frac{1}{4}$" to this figure.

For example, to compute the cut size of squares that will yield side-setting triangles for a quilt with 10" blocks:
1. Multiply the block size by 1.5: 10" x 1.5 = 15".
2. Add $1\frac{1}{4}$": 15" + $1\frac{1}{4}$" = $16\frac{1}{4}$".
3. Cut one $16\frac{1}{4}$" square, and then cut the square twice diagonally to make 4 side-setting triangles.

Use half-square triangles for the corners of diagonally set quilts. To figure the cut size of a square that will yield slightly oversized corner triangles, multiply the quilt block size by .75, and then add 1".

For example, to compute the cut size of squares that will yield corner-setting triangles for a quilt with 10" blocks:
1. Multiply the block size by .75: 10" x .75 = $7\frac{1}{2}$".
2. Add 1": $7\frac{1}{2}$" + 1" = $8\frac{1}{2}$".
3. Cut two $8\frac{1}{2}$" squares, and then cut each square once diagonally to make 4 corner triangles.

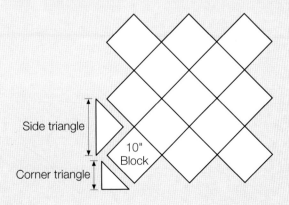

Side triangle

10" Block

Corner triangle

BASIC STITCHING

Sewing with an Accurate Seam Allowance

There is nothing more important you can do for yourself than stitch with an accurate ¼"-wide seam allowance. Since all the cutting dimensions in this book allow for ¼"-wide seam allowances, it is imperative that you sew with an accurate seam. Otherwise, small errors on each seam snowball into frustrating, inaccurate piecing. Ideally, your seams and intersections should just fall together in a perfect match.

Conduct a strip test on your machine to test both the accuracy of the ¼" seam guide and your ability to use it correctly. Cut three strips of fabric, each precisely 1½" x 3". Check the width for accuracy. Sew the strips together side by side. Align the raw edges carefully, and then sew slowly and accurately using the machine's ¼" seam guide. Press the two seam allowances away from the center strip. If properly sewn with an accurate guide, the center strip should measure precisely 1" from seam to seam.

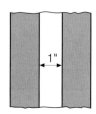

If the center strip is off by just a thread or two, check your sewing habits. Were the raw edges perfectly aligned and did you keep them that way while stitching? Did you sew too fast to keep control of the edges while stitching? Were the strips exactly 1½" wide, or were they just kind of close? Do you tend to wander when stitching as opposed to sewing a straight seam? Does your presser foot hold the fabric layers snug enough to keep them aligned, and do the feed dogs feed fabric through without shifting layers?

These little things are often the source of inaccurate seams. The solution is to slow down. Take the time to be careful and accurate when cutting and sewing. If the machine does not operate properly, get it repaired. The reduction in frustration and seam ripping are tremendous rewards for the effort.

If, despite careful stitching, the center strip does not measure exactly 1" wide, check the guide. Cut a 2" x 6" piece of ¼" graph paper. Put the paper under the presser foot and lower the needle into the paper, just barely to the right of the first ¼" grid line so that the needle is included in the dimension of the seam allowance. Otherwise, the stitching would decrease the size of the finished area by a needle's width on each seam you sew.

Adjust the paper so it runs straight forward from the needle, angling neither to the left nor to the right. Lower the presser foot to hold the paper in place. Tape the left edge of the paper down so it won't slip.

Check the machine's ¼" guide against the edge of the graph paper. If the guide is the edge of the presser foot, the edge should run perfectly along the edge of the graph paper. If the guide is an etched line on the throat plate, the same should be true. If the edge of the presser foot or etched line does not run along the edge of the graph paper, you need to make a new guide. Stick a piece of masking tape or adhesive-backed moleskin along the edge of the graph paper as shown. Make sure it is in front of and out of the way of the feed dogs. Do another strip test to check this new guide. Adjust the tape guide as necessary until you can conduct strip tests accurately several times in a row. If you are using masking tape, build up the guide with several layers of tape to create a ridge that will help you guide fabric.

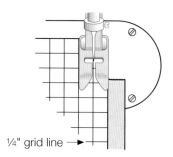

¼" grid line →

Put masking tape in front of needle along edge of graph paper to guide fabric.

Pressing

There are two primary reasons for pressing seam allowances in a particular direction: 1) to ensure that seams rest against each other (butt) at the intersections where they meet, and 2) to ensure that your completed block or quilt will lie flat and smooth. Pressing toward the darker fabric, which is a common instruction in quiltmaking, is a luxury you can consider after these two conditions have been met.

Here are a few tips for pressing a seam allowance crisply toward one side, without any pleats or puckers showing on the right side.

◆ Use a dry iron, without steam, to prevent stretching the fabric while pressing.

◆ Press, don't iron. *Pressing* is the gentle lowering, pressing, and lifting of the iron along the length of a seam; *ironing*—moving the iron forcefully back and forth along the seam—distorts it. Use an occasional spritz of water to sharply crease the fabric in the desired direction. Once damp, use only a gentle up-and-down motion to set the crease.

◆ Always press the seam line flat after sewing, before pressing the seam allowance in one direction. Pressing the seam flat relaxes and sets the thread, eases out any small puckers that result from stitching, and smoothes out any fullness you may have eased in as you stitched.

◆ Press from the right side, not from the back. Use the tip of the iron to gently press the top fabric over the seam allowance. With the seam allowance held in place by the ironing surface, it is much easier to work the larger piece of fabric over the narrower seam allowance. Pressing the seam allowance to one side from the back often results in pleats and inaccuracy on the right side. Pleats are a big problem because, as block construction and further pressing take place, the pleated seam eventually presses fully open, resulting in oversized and misshapen pieces. You must then deal with puckers, easing, and bumps in your work. Fully pressed, unpleated seams are crucial to

accuracy and are best achieved by working from the right side of the fabric where you can see and control what is happening.

◆ Press in the direction of the straight grain. When the straight grain runs along the seam, gentle pressing along the seam follows the straight grain. When the bias runs along the seam, gentle pressing at a 45° angle to the seam follows the straight grain. Do not press straight along a bias seam, or you will stretch and distort the fabric.

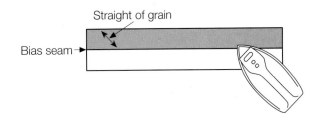

Straight of grain

Bias seam→

◆ When assembling strip units, press seams one by one as you sew them rather than waiting to press them all at once later. This doesn't mean you can't chain sew, but rather that all seams should be pressed before being joined to the next piece. It is especially critical to press each seam individually in bias strip units because seams can easily stretch if you try to manipulate and press a mass of sewn strips. You'll find that you can manage the construction of multiple strip units far better if previously sewn seams are crisply pressed and flat when you sew the next strip in place.

There are pressing instructions with each quilt plan in this book. The arrows and seam-allowance tips shown in the piecing diagrams indicate the pressing direction for each seam allowance. When arrows would be confusing, pressing instructions are indicated in the text. Be sure to follow the directions carefully. I have tried to work out the best possible pressing plan for each pattern. For in-depth information on planning seam directions for your projects, I recommend *Press for Success* by Myrna Giesbrecht.

Stitching Seams

The machine stitching called for in this book is done exclusively from raw edge to raw edge. Backstitching is unnecessary because all stitching is crossed by another seam. Even the outermost border seams are secured by the binding seam.

To join rotary-cut pieces, place them right sides together, carefully and accurately aligning the raw edges. Strips and simple piecing don't normally require pinning. It's important to sew slowly and accurately, keeping the edges aligned. Accurate cutting methods mean nothing if the stitching is not also accurate. For more information on machine piecing and rotary cutting, see my books *A Perfect Match* and *Shortcuts: A Concise Guide to Rotary Cutting.*

Matching Intersections

The easiest and most accurate way to match seam intersections is to press seam allowances that meet in opposite directions. Each of the seam allowances forms a ridge, and these ridges can be pushed tightly against each other. This is called *butting the seams*. Butting also applies to diagonal seams. If diagonal seam allowances are all pressed in the same direction where they meet, the resulting large lump makes sharp, accurate intersections and points virtually impossible. If it's impossible for all seams to butt, the second-best solution is to press the offending seam allowances open, pin them in place, and then stitch.

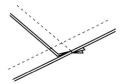

Butt straight seams.   Butt diagonal seams.

Chain Sewing

Chain sewing is an assembly-line approach to stitching. The idea is to save time and increase accuracy by sewing as many seams as possible, one right after the other, rather than stopping and starting after each unit is sewn. When you've finished sewing a set

of seams, you should have a long "kite-tail" of stitched units connected by small twists of thread. Clip the units apart and press according to the project's pressing plan.

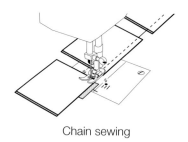

Chain sewing

Straight-Grain Strip Piecing

Straight-grain strip piecing replaces the process of cutting and sewing individual squares and rectangles. The idea is to cut strips from selvage to selvage, sew the strips together, press them, and then cut the resulting strip unit into segments. These strip units can be simple or complex depending on the demands of the pattern. The simple Nine Patch is a good example of basic straight-grain strip piecing.

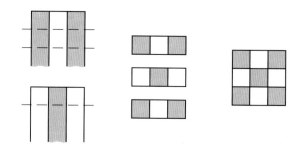

Checking Your Work

As you stitch, it's a good idea to check the dimensions of the units you have just sewn to make sure they are the correct size. It is much easier to correct problems at each stage of construction rather than later when ripping seams and restitching become complicated, and time-consuming. Interior pieces should measure the intended finished size, and outer pieces should measure the finished size plus 1/2" for seam allowances. Check one last time when the blocks are complete. Rip and restitch or trim units to size as necessary.

BIAS STRIP PIECING

Bias strip piecing is similar to straight-grain strip piecing except that the strips are cut on the bias instead of the straight grain of the fabric. Why cut strips on the bias? A look at the most common unit cut from bias strip units, the bias square, reveals the answer. The bias square is traditionally composed of two half-square triangles sewn together on their long bias edges. Consequently, the straight grain lies on the edge of the square.

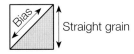

If you cut squares from straight-grain strip units, the outer edges of the squares will have bias edges. But if you cut squares from bias-cut strip units, the outer edges of the square will have straight-grain edges.

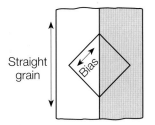
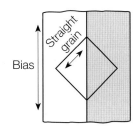

You can use bias strip piecing to make many other types of units. The beauty of the method is that there are no small pieces to work with; all the sewing and pressing is done before the final unit is cut, resulting in perfect, distortion-free units every time.

Side-by-Side

Regular-Stripe

Center-Stripe Square

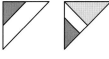
Striped Triangles

Striped Rectangle

Cutting Bias Strips

The Bias Stripper ruler makes cutting bias strips easy. It looks different from standard rulers so that it will not be confused with them. Its longest edge has a ½" margin to account for the two seams on either side of a bias strip. Measurements are marked in ⅛" increments along the two short edges of the ruler, and continuous lines run the length of the ruler every inch. Other lines run parallel to the ruler's short edges. The ruler is easy for both left-handed and right-handed quilters to use. Cutting distances on the Bias Stripper are referred to as "cutting marks."

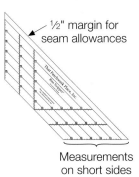

½" margin for seam allowances

Measurements on short sides

Several layers of fabric can be cut into bias strips at the same time, but it is important for all the fabrics to be layered in the same direction, either all print-side up or all print-side down. If not, you will end up with strips that slant in opposite directions. Since the final slant of the strip unit itself does not matter unless you are making striped rectangles, consistency in fabric direction (whether all up or all down) is the important factor.

1. Lay the fabric on the cutting mat with the short edges to the left and right as shown. Do not fold the fabric. To make the first cut, align the short edge of the Bias Stripper ruler with the upper corner of the fabric. Cut the fabric along the edge of the ruler from bottom to top. Set aside the corner piece created by this first cut.

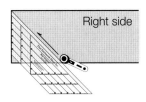

Right side

Right-handed

2. Cut bias strips from the fabric by aligning the required cutting mark on the short edges of the Bias Stripper with the cut edge of the fabric.

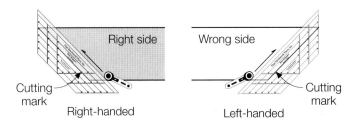

Cutting mark
Right side
Right-handed

Wrong side
Cutting mark
Left-handed

3. Continue cutting bias strips until you can no longer cut full strips (strips that run completely from top to bottom). There will be another corner piece left over

at this side of the fabric. Sometimes, the last full bias strip will be just a little short (clipped) on the lower corner. You can use the clipped strip as long as the clipped point is less than 1" high. Do not cut the last strip into a clipped strip if it will have a clip higher than 1".

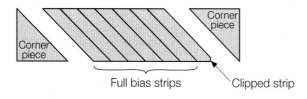

Full bias strips   Clipped strip

Tip

You can cut the corner triangles into corner bias strips to use for simple units, such as bias squares or side-by-sides. Otherwise, set them aside for use in another project.

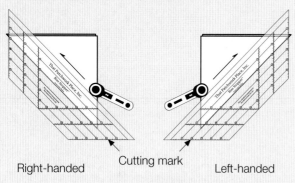

Right-handed   Cutting mark   Left-handed

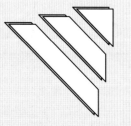

When cutting bias strips from leftover corner triangles, first trim any extra fabric from the second triangle you created.

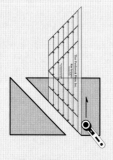

Trim off extra fabric
from second triangle.

Sewing Bias Strip Units

You can sew full and corner bias strips into many types of units.

Full Bias Strip Units

Sew together only full bias strips to make full bias strip units. Use this type of unit to cut any type of bias unit, from bias squares to striped rectangles. Organize the strips as indicated in the pattern diagram. If you are using clipped strips, lay the clipped ends toward the bottom edge of the unit. Working either from left to right or right to left, sew the strips into pairs, then the pairs into fours, and so on, following the directions below.

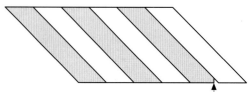

Put clipped strips on bottom of strip unit.

◆ Sew with an accurate ¼"-wide seam allowance. If your seam allowance isn't accurate, your finished units will not meet other units as they should along the edges. Diagonal seams that should match will "miss" each other. Take the time to learn how to consistently sew an accurate seam allowance to avoid disappointing results. See "Sewing with an Accurate Seam Allowance" on page 10.

◆ Offset the strips when sewing. Begin stitching at the V, where the angled edges of the two strips intersect at the ¼"-wide seam allowance. This yields a strip unit that is even along the upper edge, making it easy to cut into squares and rectangles. If you do not offset the strips properly, your strip units will resemble a stepladder, which is wasteful and difficult to cut.

Offset strips
so ¼" seam
starts at V.

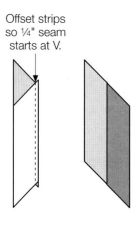

◈ Always sew strips from the top of the strip unit to the bottom so that the upper edge of the unit is even.

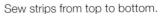

Sew strips from top to bottom.

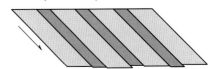

◈ Sew slowly and carefully, handling the strips as little as possible to prevent stretching. Sewing slowly is very important. Align the bias edges, and use a seam ripper and a light touch to guide the strips, letting the feed dogs pull the strips along.

◈ If the edges of your bias strips tend to separate as you sew, despite your best efforts to control them, the problem may be with the presser foot. In most cases, switching to a wider foot that completely covers the feed dogs solves the problem. Of course, if you are using the edge of your presser foot as the ¼" guide, you will need to make a new guide. (See "Sewing with an Accurate Seam Allowance" on page 10 for help with creating a new guide.) If the wider foot doesn't help, take the machine to a service center for assistance.

◈ If you need to take out a bias seam, use a seam ripper to cut the thread every two to three stitches on one side, and then lift the bias strips apart. Other ripping methods can stretch the bias edges.

◈ Press each seam before adding another strip to the unit. Pressing all the seams at once after the strip unit is sewn will result in badly stretched, poorly pressed seams. See "Pressing" on page 11 for proper pressing methods. Follow the pressing instructions provided with each pattern.

Corner Bias Strip Units

Use bias strips cut from leftover corner triangles to make corner bias strip units. Use corner bias strip units to make simple bias units without stripes, such as bias squares and side-by-sides. When you don't have enough leftover corner triangles, cut large squares of fabric into half-square triangles.

Pair the strips right sides together, aligning the bias edge and the upper point. Stitch along the long bias edges slowly and carefully, sewing from the top

of the strip to the bottom. Press according to the pattern directions.

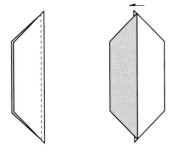

Sew the strip pairs into multiple strip units, keeping the units together according to length and aligning the points on one edge. Remember to press each seam before sewing a piece to another unit.

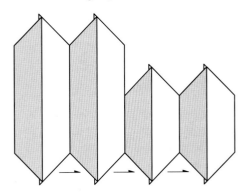

Combination Bias Strip Units

When you need large quantities of bias squares or side-by-side units, combine full and corner bias strips into units. Follow the assembly guidelines for full bias strip units, being careful to offset all strips so the top edge of the strip unit is even.

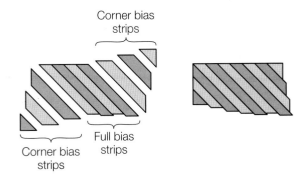

Corner bias strips

Corner bias strips

Full bias strips

Cutting Bias Squares and Side-by-Sides

Cut bias squares ½" larger than desired finished size. Use a Bias Square ruler to cut bias squares from sewn and pressed strip units. The Bias Square ruler has a diagonal line and ⅛" markings that meet at the center to form squares.

A *side-by-side* is nothing more than a bias square cut in half on the diagonal—two pieced half-square triangles. Cut side-by-sides just as you would a bias square. The only difference is in the cut size of the square. Since a side-by-side is the same as a half-square triangle, the bias square needs to be ⅞" larger than the desired finished size of the side-by-side. Note that the two side-by-sides cut from one bias square are mirror-image units.

Finished size + ⅞"

Side-by-Sides

Bias squares can be cut from any of the three different types of bias strip units. Follow the instructions below to cut bias squares from full, combination, or corner bias strip units.

Full Bias Strip Units

1. Assemble the strip unit as instructed in the quilt pattern. Position the strip unit on the cutting mat with the even edge toward you. Angle the unit to the left or right as comfort dictates, just as you might with a piece of writing paper.

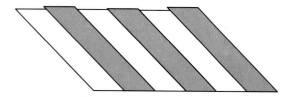

2. Center the diagonal line of the Bias Square ruler on the seam closest to the pointed end of the strip unit. If the strip unit slants to the left, the pointed end will be on the right and you will cut from right to left. If the strip unit slants to the right, the opposite will be true. Keep the desired cutting mark above the bottom raw edge of the strip unit. Cut the top and side of the bias square from raw edge to raw edge.

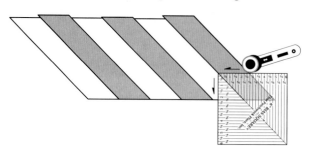

3. Turn the fabric and align the proper markings on the Bias Square ruler with the clean-cut edges. Make sure the ruler's diagonal line is aligned with the seam, then trim the two remaining raw edges to the desired size.

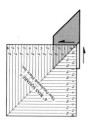

4. Continue cutting bias squares from right to left or left to right, depending on the slant of the strip unit. There will always be tiny slivers of waste fabric between each bias square and leftover edge triangles along the raw edges of the strip unit.

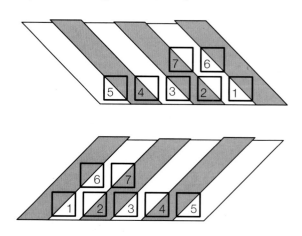

Combination Bias Strip Units

Cut bias squares from combination strip units just as you would from a full strip unit. The only difference is that there will be no leftover edge triangles.

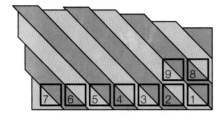

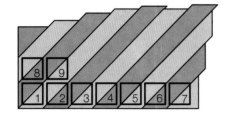

Corner Bias Strip Units

1. Align the even points of the strip unit toward you. Position the unit at an angle as necessary for comfort. Begin with the lower point on either the left or right. Position the diagonal line of the Bias Square ruler on the seam with the desired dimensions above the raw edges. Cut the top two edges of the bias square from raw edge to raw edge.

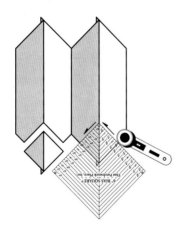

2. Turn the bias square and trim the raw edges to the desired size.

3. Continue cutting across the bottom of the strip unit, moving from lowest point to lowest point as indicated by the cutting order in the illustration. There will be leftover edge triangles and tiny slivers of waste fabric between bias squares.

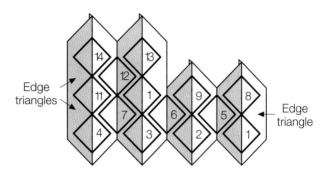

Cutting Striped Squares and Striped Triangles

Striped squares are similar to bias squares except they have one or more interior stripes running across the bias. As with any square use the Bias Square ruler to cut these ½" larger than the desired finished size. There are two types of striped squares: regular-stripe squares, which have one or more stripes on one side of the center seam, and center-stripe squares, which have a diagonal middle stripe and no center seam.

Regular-Stripe
Square

Center-Stripe
Square

Cut striped triangles as you would side-by-sides, by cutting a striped square into two half-square triangles. Just as with side-by-sides, the cut size of the striped square needs to be ⅞" larger than the desired finished size of the triangles.

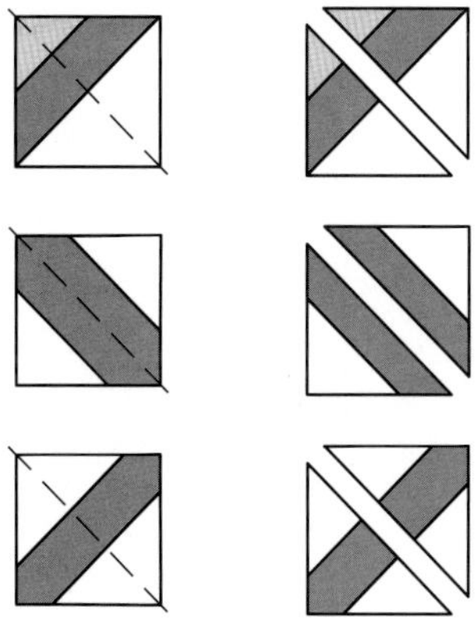

Make strip units for striped squares and triangles from full bias strips only. You'd waste a lot of fabric if you cut these units from leftover corner triangles; I prefer to save corner triangles for bias squares. To cut striped squares, follow the procedures for cutting bias squares from full bias strip units, with the following exceptions:

Regular-Stripe Squares

Align the diagonal line of the Bias Square ruler with the seam that will run through the center of the square. Be careful not to confuse this seam with any others in the strip unit.

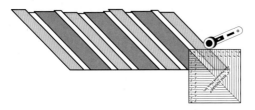

There will be small waste rectangles between pairs of striped squares and leftover edge triangles.

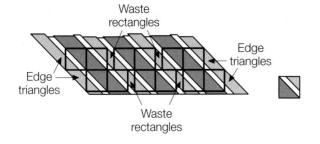

Center-Stripe Squares

1. Draw a chalk line through the center of each strip that will run through the middle of the block. To determine the center mark, divide the cutting mark for the center strip in half. For example, if the cutting mark is 2", half of that is the 1" mark. Measure from the seam to the center of the strip by counting increments from the nonmargin edge of the Bias Stripper. Ignore the numbers printed on the ruler. Just remember the bold lines are 1" marks and the lighter lines in between are ⅛" increments. Look closely at the illustration; it shows the proper orientation of the Bias Stripper. The patterns in this book give measurements for finding the center.

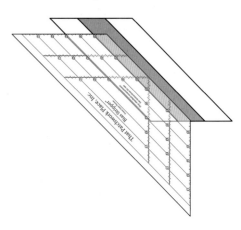

As an alternative to measuring, fold each strip in half, matching seams, and press to mark the center. Mark the crease by using a ruler and a chalk pencil. I find that rolling chalk wheels work best.

2. Cut center-stripe squares by using the chalk line as the guide for the diagonal line on the Bias Square ruler.

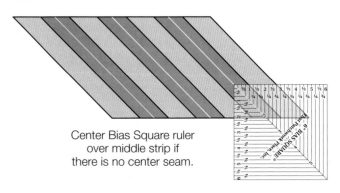

Center Bias Square ruler over middle strip if there is no center seam.

Cutting Striped Rectangles

Striped rectangles are rectangles that have stripes running across the true bias. Because they have bias seams, you need to cut them from full bias strip units. Striped rectangles slant either to the left or to the right depending on the pattern; therefore, so do the strip units used to make the rectangles. Assemble and position the full bias strip unit as indicated in the pattern. To produce rectangles that slant correctly, you must be careful to cut the bias strips from fabric that is facing the proper direction, either print-side up or print-side down. If you are left-handed, pay attention to the specific directions for reversing print direction.

Use a standard rotary ruler or Mary Hickey's BiRangle ruler to cut rectangles from the strip unit. If you are using a standard quilter's ruler, it should be at least 6" wide and marked with a 1" grid and ⅛" markings along each grid line. Some people find it helpful to mark off the rectangle they are cutting with ¼"-wide masking tape on the ruler. If you use the BiRangle ruler, ignore the diagonal line; it is a guide for another technique. Depending on the slant of the strip unit you are cutting, you might need to use the BiRangle ruler either face up or face down.

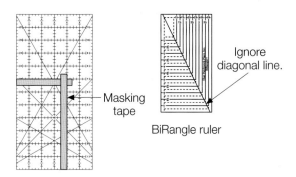

Standard quilter's ruler

BiRangle ruler

Masking tape

Ignore diagonal line.

1. Angle the strip unit as necessary for comfortable cutting, with the even edge toward you. Position the ruler on a full bias strip unit, with the rectangular dimensions above the lower raw edge. For left-facing strip units, align the upper left corner of the ruler with the seam of what will be the upper left corner of the rectangle (arrow A). The opposite lower right corner of the rectangle should be aligned with the seam that intersects the corner on that side of the rectangle (arrow B). Reverse the procedure for right-facing strip units, moving the masking tape markers to the opposite side of the ruler or turning the BiRangle ruler over. Depending on the number of interior stripes, one or more seams may fall between the two that intersect the rectangle corners. Shift the ruler as necessary to align points A and B. Don't worry about the placement of the interior seams or whether the lower edge of the ruler or markings are parallel with the lower edge of the strip unit. The only thing that matters is properly aligning points A and B on the seam lines.

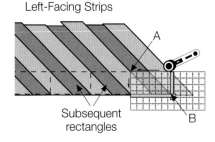

Left-Facing Strips

A

Subsequent rectangles

B

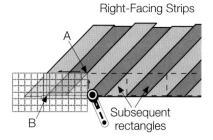

Right-Facing Strips

A

B

Subsequent rectangles

2. Cut 2 sides of the rectangle. Don't cut too far into the strip unit when cutting the short side, or you will cut into the rectangles to be cut above. Cutting ⅛" to ¼" above the ruler is okay.

3. Turn the rectangle around and trim the remaining two sides to the desired size.

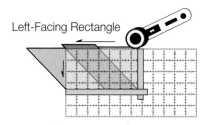

Left-Facing Rectangle

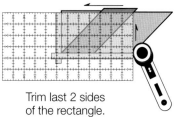

Right-Facing Rectangle

Trim last 2 sides of the rectangle.

4. Continue cutting rectangles across the bottom of the strip unit. There will be small slivers of waste between the rectangles and leftover edge triangles.

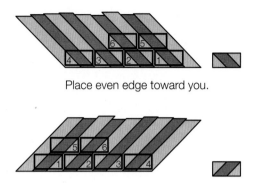

Place even edge toward you.

Determining Bias Strip Widths

Cut widths for bias strips are provided for each pattern in this book. To determine bias strip widths for other projects, it is important to understand the two types of strips that make up bias squares and the assorted striped units. *Corner strips* are the strips that make up the two triangular corners of any bias unit. *Interior strips* are any strips that run through the middle of a unit between the two corner strips. Bias squares and side-by-sides have only corner strips because they are each made up of two triangles. Striped bias units have two corner strips with one or more interior strips between them.

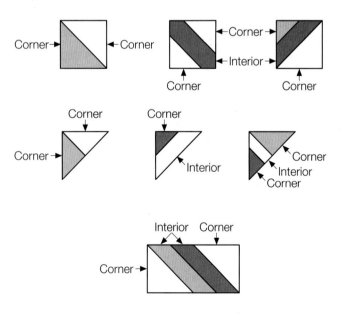

The cutting marks on the Bias Stripper indicate the desired finished size of bias strips where they fall at the edge of a unit. It is important that interior strips measure evenly along the side of the unit, as opposed to across the strip's width, so that they can match other patchwork pieces.

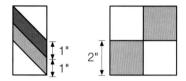

The following chart shows how much to add to the finished size (FS) to get the Bias Stripper cutting mark for corner and interior bias strips.

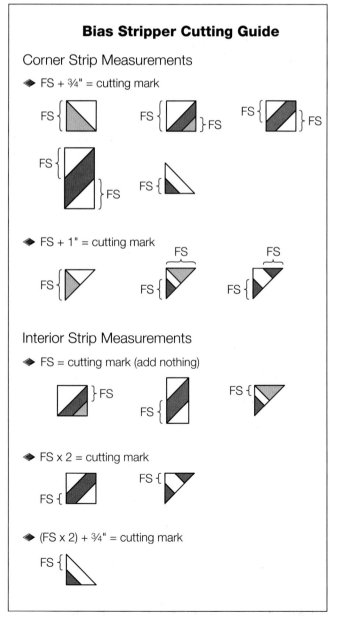

MAKING STRIP UNITS FOR BIAS SQUARES

When designing your own projects or adapting existing patterns to bias strip piecing, it helps to know how to make bias strip units. It's not as difficult as you may think. All you need to know to get started is how many bias squares you want to cut and how big you want to cut them. From that, you can design a simple strip unit and figure the size of fabric pieces you need for cutting bias strips for the unit.

To illustrate, we will design and figure fabric and cutting requirements for 40 bias squares that finish to 2" (2½" cut size). From the Bias Stripper Cutting Guide shown previously, we know to cut bias strips for 2" finished-size bias squares at the 2¾" mark on the Bias Stripper ruler.

Designing the Bias Strip Unit

1. Draw 40 squares on graph paper in a 4 x 10 grid. Use 1 graph square for each bias square.

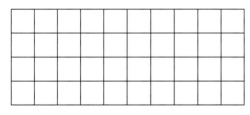

4 x 10 grid

2. Draw diagonal lines through the grid to make the bias squares. Color in every other diagonal stripe. You now have a rough drawing of the bias strip unit you need. Identify the number of full bias strips in the drawing. In this case, there are 3 light and 3 dark full bias strips. You now have all the information you need to figure the fabric sizes that will yield enough bias strips for this unit.

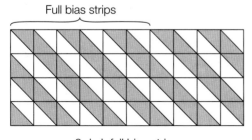

Full bias strips

3 dark full bias strips
3 light full bias strips

Determining Fabric and Cutting Requirements

To understand how to figure fabric width and length, it helps to look at how we cut bias strips. In the illustration below, you can see the fabric piece we need and how it will be cut into bias strips. The fabric width must accommodate the number of rows you drew—in this case, 4. The fabric length must accommodate the size of each full bias strip along the bottom edge of the fabric (strip base) plus the size of the corner triangle. It doesn't matter whether you will cut the corner triangle into bias strips.

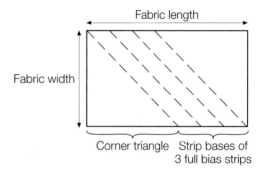

Fabric length

Fabric width

Corner triangle   Strip bases of 3 full bias strips

1. Figure fabric width by multiplying the number of rows in the strip unit by bias square size. In this case, we have four rows of 2½" bias squares, so 2½" x 4 = 10" for perfect fabric width. But we are not perfect, so always add 2" to this measurement to provide for loss from sewing and wiggle room. In this example, you would cut the fabric 12" wide. Note that the short side of the corner triangle will equal the fabric width.

Tip

TRY TO AVOID CUTTING FABRIC PIECES WIDER THAN 12", AND I LIMIT THE NUMBER OF ROWS IN MY STRIP UNITS ACCORDINGLY. I FIND STRIP UNITS WIDER THAN 12" UNWIELDY AND PRONE TO STRETCHING.

2. Fabric length depends on the size of the corner triangle, the number of full bias strips, and the strip-base size. In this example, we need 3 full bias strips from each print, each cut at the 2¾" mark. *Strip base always equals cutting mark plus ¾"*. So, in our example, 2¾" + ¾" = 3½" strip base. Multiply the number of full bias strips by the strip base to get the total strip base: 3 x 3½" = 10½". Add the corner-triangle size to the total strip base to get the fabric length: 10½" + 12" = 22½". In this example, you would cut the fabric 22½" long.

Total fabric size is width x length, or 12" x 22½". Since you need the same number of bias strips in the same size from the second print, the fabric size is the same. Cut fabric pieces to this size, and then cut full and corner bias strips at the 2¾" mark to make the strip unit you designed. You'll even have a few leftover corner strips to provide for any shortages.

To make it even easier, here is a Bias Strip Unit Work Sheet you can use to figure fabric size for each print in a bias strip unit. To use the work sheet, first draw your grid, and then plug in the numbers in each step. You'll have your fabric requirements when done. You may copy this work sheet for yourself any time you need to design a bias strip unit. Use one work sheet for each print used in the strip unit.

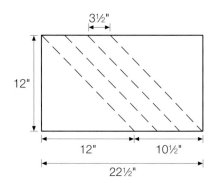

Bias Strip Unit Work Sheet

A. Number of bias squares: _____

B. Finished size of bias square: _____

C. Bias-strip cutting mark (B + ¾"): _____

D. Cut size of bias square (B + ½"): _____

E. Number of rows (see your grid): _____

F. Fabric width (D x E) plus 2": _____

G. Strip base (C + ¾"): _____

H. Number of full bias strips
   needed (see grid): _____

I. Fabric length (G x H) + F: _____

   Fabric Size (F by I): _____

OTHER USES FOR THE BIAS STRIPPER

In many block designs and piecing situations, it is desirable for squares to measure evenly across the diagonal as opposed to along the edge. A good example is shown below, a Nine Patch block set on point in the center of a traditional Variable Star. How wide would you rotary-cut the squares to make the Nine Patch block? There is no easy answer, since the desirable situation is for the squares to measure evenly across the diagonal to fit in with the rest of the block (2" across each square in the example below). If we use a standard rotary ruler when cutting squares, we can't measure the distance across the center diagonal. The solution in the past has been to draft and use full-size templates, individually cutting each piece.

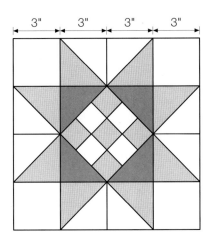

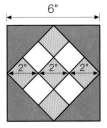

To fit, nine-patch squares should measure 2" across the diagonal.

The same problems exist for bias squares set on point.

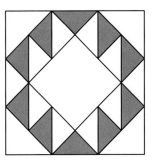

Bias Squares should measure evenly across the diagonal.

Another frequent use of on-point construction is in pieced borders and seminole piecing. In the past, figuring how to fit borders like these onto a quilt was a daunting project.

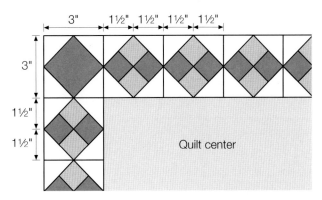

You want even measurements across the diagonal of squares so the border fits the quilt center.

The Bias Stripper is the answer to all these piecing difficulties. The ruler's cutting marks are the even diagonals of squares and strips, making it the perfect tool for creating units that measure evenly across the diagonal. The Bias Stripper makes it easy to rotary cut and strip piece accurately sized squares and bias squares set on point.

Making On-Point Squares and Straight-Grain Strip Units

Use the Bias Stripper to cut squares and strips for straight-grain strip piecing. Follow normal procedures for cutting squares and strips. The only thing that changes is the tool you use to do the job. To cut on-point squares:

1. Determine the desired finished diagonal measurement of the square.
2. Using the Bias Stripper, cut straight-grain strips at that mark.
3. Turn the strips and cut squares at the same mark.

It's that simple; the cutting mark equals the finished diagonal measurement. The ½" margin on the edge of the ruler provides for the seam allowances on either side of the square or strip.

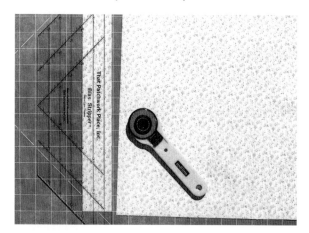

To strip piece simple straight-set units, such as a Nine Patch, use the Bias Stripper to cut straight-grain strips, and then sew the strips into units as you would normally. Again, the process is the same, only the tool is different. Cut strips at the mark that equals the diagonal of the finished square. For example, to strip-piece a Nine Patch:

1. Determine the desired finished diagonal measurement of the squares.
2. Using the Bias Stripper, cut straight-grain strips at that mark.

TIP
After every third or fourth cut, use a standard ruler to check that the seams are still at right angles to the cutting edge. Place one of the ruler's horizontal lines on the seam and one of the vertical lines on the cut edge.

3. Sew the strips into a unit and cut it into segments at the same mark, using the Bias Stripper.

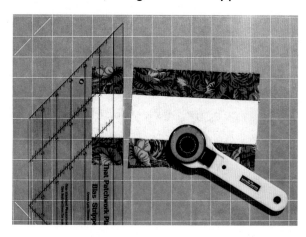

Making Bias Strip Units for On-Point Bias Squares

Use standard bias strip-piecing techniques to cut on-point bias squares, but reverse the use of the tools. Use a regular ruler to cut the bias strips and the Bias Stripper to cut the bias squares. To cut bias squares on point:

1. Determine the desired finished diagonal measurement of the bias square.

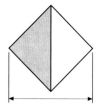

Finished bias square
diagonal (3")

2. Divide the diagonal measurement in half and add 1". Using a standard rotary ruler, cut bias strips to this width. For example, if you want a bias square that measures 3" across the diagonal, divide 3" in half (1½") and add 1" (1½" + 1" = 2½"). Using a standard rotary ruler, cut bias strips 2½" wide.
3. Assemble the bias strip unit as you would normally.
4. Rather than cut individual bias squares from the strip unit, use the Bias Stripper to cut short vertical segments. The cutting mark equals the desired finished diagonal measurement of the bias squares. For example, if you want bias squares that measure 3" across the diagonal, use the 3" cutting mark.

5. Orient the bias strip unit horizontally on the cutting mat, with the even edge at the top of the strip unit. Position the Bias Stripper vertically with the long margin edge ¼" to the right of the second seam on the upper edge of the strip unit. Position a diagonal line of the ruler on one of the seams at the same time. (If you are left-handed, position the ruler from the right side of the strip unit, with the margin edge ¼" to the right of the first seam on the upper edge and a diagonal ruler line on the seam.)

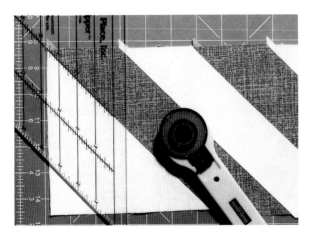

6. Cut along the edge of the Bias Stripper to make a vertical segment. Continue cutting vertical segments as described previously, up to the last cut from the last seam on the top. There will still be a big piece left to be cut into 2 more segments.

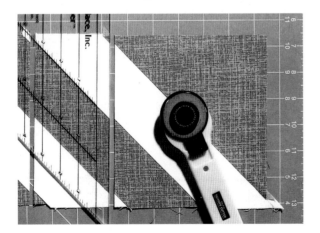

7. To cut the last big piece, position the ruler vertically as before, with the diagonal line on one of the seams and the margin edge ¼" to the left of the seam on the bottom. Cut a vertical segment.

The last uncut segment can be cut directly to size at the desired cutting mark.

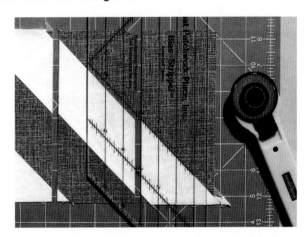

8. Turn the remaining segments 180° and trim. Align the desired cutting mark with the clean-cut edge and place a diagonal line on the seam. Trim the opposite edge of the segment.

9. Place the diagonal line of the Bias Stripper on the first seam in the segment so that the upper edge of the ruler falls exactly at the top left point of the seam. The cutting mark should be on the lower right seam corner. Cut along the upper edge of the ruler to cut the bias square.

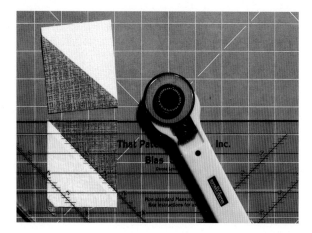

10. Turn the bias square around and trim it to the cutting mark. With the cutting mark on the lower clean-cut edge, place one of the ruler's diagonal lines on the seam. Trim the excess fabric above the ruler's edge. Continue cutting bias squares from the segments in the same manner. There will be small slivers of waste between each bias square.

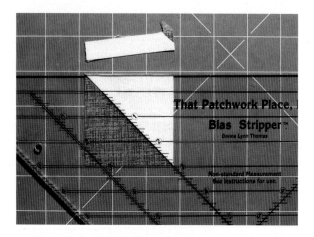

To summarize on-point construction:

◆ Using the Bias Stripper, cut all squares, strips, and bias squares at the mark equal to the desired finished diagonal measurement of the unit.

◆ Use a standard rotary ruler when cutting bias strips for on-point construction. Strip width equals half the finished diagonal measurement plus 1".

◆ Use a standard rotary ruler to cut the bias strips and a Bias Stripper ruler to cut the bias squares.

Cutting Diamonds

Using the Bias Stripper to cut diamonds eliminates the need to make a paper-template cutting guide.

1. Determine the desired finished size of the diamond along an edge. As with a square, all edges of the diamond are the same length. Cut straight-grain strips at this mark using the Bias Stripper.

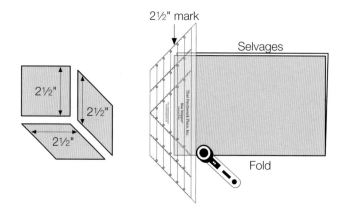

2. Unfold the strip. Align the Bias Stripper on the strip as shown and trim one end to a 45° angle.

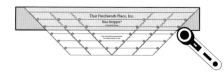

3. Turn the strip and cut diamonds from it at the same mark you used when you cut the strips. Align the ruler on both the cutting edge and the top raw edge of the strip at the same time. Retrim the end of the strip if you can't align the ruler exactly on both edges.

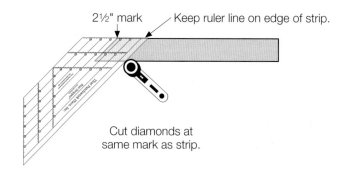

Cut diamonds at
same mark as strip.

GALLERY

AMISH PUZZLE

DONNA LYNN THOMAS, 1996, PEACHTREE CITY, GEORGIA, 62¾" x 62¾". QUILTED BY JUDY KELLER.

Simplicity of color and design are the earmarks of Amish quilts. Despite that, I couldn't help spicing up the border and binding. Judy quilted beautifully with different colors of thread. The end result is an Amish twist on the traditional Yankee Puzzle block. Directions begin on page 73.

GAUDETE

LINDA KITTLE, 1996, LEAVENWORTH, KANSAS, 66¼" x 66¼".

Linda admits that the inspiration for her colors came while she was daydreaming during mass one Sunday. Admiring the richness of the church decorations, she decided to model her quilt after the colors of the liturgical season. Then, being musically inclined, she quilted musical instruments and motifs in the open spaces. The result, "Gaudete" (rejoice), is a beautiful quilt.

Bob's Lost Ships

Donna Lynn Thomas, 1996, Peachtree City, Georgia, 51" x 51". Quilted by Ann Woodward.

The traditional Lost Ships block seemed the perfect way to remember my beloved cousin, Robert Clayton, lost in a whitewater rafting accident in June 1995. There are forty-one ships, one for each year of his life, made from all the beautiful colors of the water he loved. The quilted sunbursts in each block celebrate the joy and exuberance with which he lived each year. The quilted trees and waves are reminders of the outdoors, where he spent his happiest times. Directions begin on page 40.

Indigo Armada

Dee Glenn, 1996, Lansing, Kansas, 77⅜" x 77⅜".

The simple two-print palette creates a stunning quilt. Notice the white ship reflected in the water below each blue ship— ah, but four little ships are out of formation! Dee's lovely machine quilting and the corded finish add depth, softness, and movement to the overall design.

BATHTUB FLOTILLA

DONNA LYNN THOMAS, 1996, PEACHTREE CITY, GEORGIA, 32⅜" x 41". QUILTED BY KARI LANE.

Bright colors and whimsy make this a perfect quilt for a child's bedroom. Think of the great adventures that could take place among the quilted whales and stars. The two-blocks-at-a-time approach makes it easy to make this quilt any size you wish— even bed-size to enhance dreams of pirate conquest.

APPLE ORCHARD

SALLY SCHNEIDER, 1996, MILL CREEK, WASHINGTON, 56⅝" x 56⅝".

Hmm…crisp red apples on green-leaved trees under blue skies. This cheerful quilt would warm the heart any time of year with visions of summer. The different green prints make the trees appear to shimmer in sunshine. Directions begin on page 45.

Tile Puzzle

Kari Lane, 1996, Lawson, Missouri, 67" x 91".

Reminiscent of mosaic tiles, Kari's inspired fabric selections bring this simple design to life. Careful color placement creates a basket-weave effect. Kari used the Bias Stripper while cutting the on-point border squares, which measure exactly 2" across the diagonal for a perfect fit. Directions begin on page 80.

Desert Dogs

Deb Rose, 1996, Fort Leavenworth, Kansas, 55¼" x 55¼".

Deb really stretched beyond her usual color choices in this quilt, with marvelous success. Unable to resist the teal dachshund print, Deb worked from there into wonderful southwestern colors. Molly, Deb's little dachshund, probably will not be allowed to burrow under this quilt, but she should feel honored to be the inspiration for such a fun piece! Directions begin on page 69.

STARWEAVE

DONNA LYNN THOMAS, 1994,
LANSING, KANSAS, 60½" x 60½".
QUILTED BY ANN WOODWARD.

Warm colors of the hearth weave quietly across the surface of this quilt. A secondary design appears where the blocks meet at the corners. Directions begin on page 77.

PANSY PATCH

DONNA LYNN THOMAS, 1996,
PEACHTREE CITY, GEORGIA,
61" x 61". QUILTED BY ALINE DUERR
AND NORMA JEAN ROHMAN.

In my Georgia town, pansies are planted in the fall and bloom right up until summer. Their cheerful purple and yellow faces brighten the landscape until the Bambi brigade comes to munch at the winter buffet so graciously provided. Even so, pansies are a favorite and, of course, a choice subject for a quilt. Change the colors to suit yourself, and bring a garden inside. Directions begin on page 61.

WHO's THAT NEIGHBOR?

KARI LANE, 1996, LAWSON, MISSOURI, 52" x 60".

Kari's talent is in taking a pattern and presenting it in a unique way. Black backgrounds showcase her extensive collection of batiks and beautiful hand-dyed and -painted fabrics. What a glorious feast for the eyes!

CENTENNIAL

BETH RHODES, 1996, SAN DIEGO, CALIFORNIA, 44" x 52".

Beth chose reproduction prints to commemorate her ancestors' emigration to the United States from Lithuania. The simplicity of design delights the eyes and recalls times past. To complete her quilt, Beth transferred an old family photo to muslin and attached it to the back of her quilt, along with some family history. What a treasured heirloom!

Next Door Neighbor

Donna Lynn Thomas, 1996,
Peachtree City, Georgia,
54½" x 62½". Quilted by
Kari Lane.

Another quilt built two blocks at a time— this traditional block is easy to make in a rainbow of colors. Dig into your fabric stash and play! Kari's sparkling quilting livens the surface and makes it shine. Directions begin on page 42.

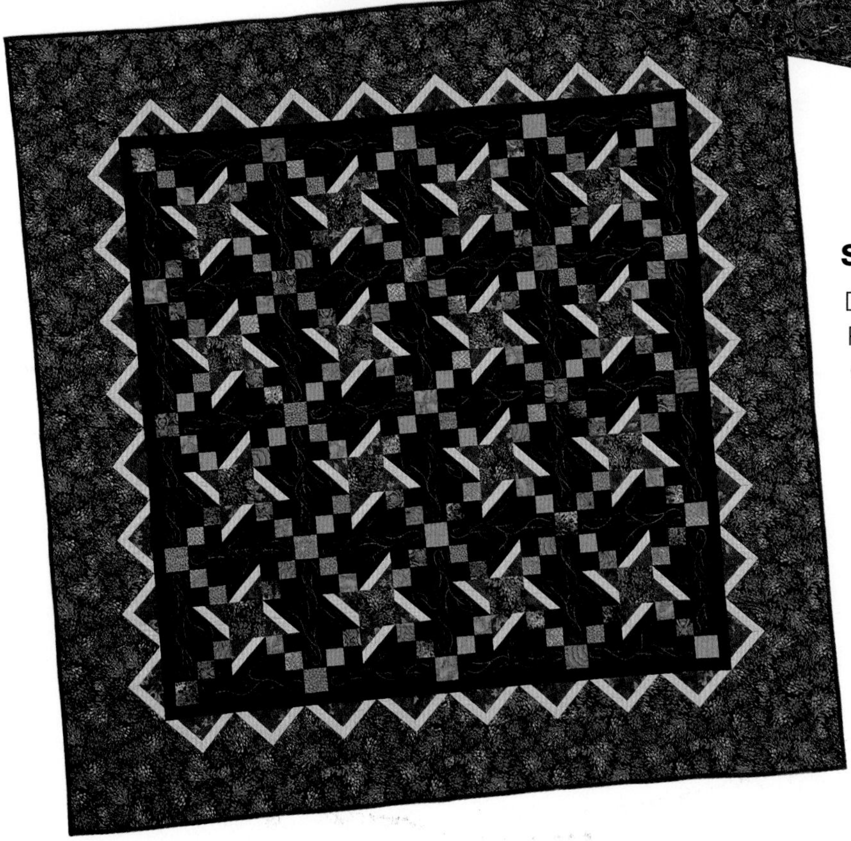

Star of Destiny

Donna Lynn Thomas, 1996,
Peachtree City, Georgia, 65½" x 65½".
Quilted by Betty Gilliam.

Bright, clear colors shine against black. The exquisite vines quilted in the sashing beautifully complement the simple blocks. Directions begin on page 49.

STARLIGHT EXPRESS

LINDA KITTLE, 1996, LEAVENWORTH, KANSAS, 50" x 50".

I'm sure Linda's choice of bright, clear colors and soft pink inspired the name for her quilt. The pink border background gives this elegant quilt a different look. Directions begin on page 85.

VARIABLE SQUARES

DONNA LYNN THOMAS, 1996, PEACHTREE CITY, GEORGIA, 50" x 50". QUILTED BY KARI LANE.

Adaptations of the traditional Variable Stars, these blocks are loaded with on-point squares and bias squares. The blocks are set together with pieced sashing strips so they appear to overlap at the corners. I chose smoky reds, grays, and blues and floated the border's on-point squares on the light background.

TOAD IN A PUDDLE

DONNA LYNN THOMAS, 1996, PEACHTREE CITY, GEORGIA, 31½" x 31½". QUILTED BY KARI LANE.

Just the name of this delightful old design meant I couldn't resist. Updating it with modern on-point construction techniques resulted in squares and bias squares that measure evenly across the diagonal. I coordinated the fabrics with the floral print. Directions begin on page 83.

REVERIE

BETH WAGENAAR, 1996, HINESVILLE, GEORGIA, 43" x 51".

Beth's passion for antique quilts is made obvious by her choice of rich, warm reproduction prints. Because she placed her values differently, Beth's Toad in the Puddle blocks look different from mine, shown above. With a fine pieced border and beautiful hand stippling, Beth's quilt truly inspires long moments of quiet reverie.

SWEET GARDENS IN THE STARS

GABRIEL PURSELL, 1996,
LEAVENWORTH, KANSAS,
68⅛" x 85⅛". QUILTED BY ALINE
DUERR AND NORMA JEAN ROHMAN.

You can tell that this lovely, romantic quilt was made by a gardener. The delicate florals make me think of a gracious afternoon tea in the garden. Notice that although the eighteen blocks are set on point, the design appears to be a straight set. Directions begin on page 52.

SORBET STARS

ROBIN CHAMBERS, 1996,
MEDIA, PENNSYLVANIA, 67" x 67".

Robin made her bright and happy quilt from many different prints. We both chose to make only sixteen blocks for our quilts—mine was "English Lady," shown opposite—and set them straight for a deceptively on-point appearance.

STAR CROSSED

DEB ROSE, 1996, FORT LEAVENWORTH, KANSAS, 58½" x 82½".

Deb used deep, rich colors in her quilt to glorious effect. Although intricate in appearance, the quilt is actually a straight set with pieced sashing strips that create the effect of overlapping blocks. Deb's perfect hand quilting adds to the beauty of this lovely piece. Directions begin on page 64.

ENGLISH LADY

DONNA LYNN THOMAS, 1996,
PEACHTREE CITY, GEORGIA, 62" x 62".
QUILTED BY CHARLOTTE FREEMAN.

Nothing is more relaxing than a day spent in the garden. Because I have a passion for perennial gardening, I am drawn to large-scale floral prints. I coordinated the fabrics in this garden quilt with the lovely rose print.

SLEIGHT OF HAND

DONNA LYNN THOMAS, 1996,
PEACHTREE CITY, GEORGIA,
24½" x 24½". QUILTED BY KARI LANE.

Warm reds and rich blues will find a place on my walls anytime. The name for this little wall hanging comes from the fact that the block is a variation on the traditional Card Tricks block, hence "sleight of hand." It would be easy to make more block quartets and increase the size of this quilt. Directions begin on page 56.

INTERLOCKIN'

DONNA LYNN THOMAS, 1996,
PEACHTREE CITY, GEORGIA,
24½" x 24½". QUILTED BY
JUDY KELLER.

The black background underscores the vibrancy of the teal and purple prints chosen by my mother, Mary Lou Brooks. Although she's never made a quilt, she's an expert seamstress with an excellent sense of color and design. My husband thought the blocks looked like interlocking chains, and so the quilt was named.

THE PATTERNS

Now we get to the fun stuff! The patterns are rated from one cutter to three cutters to indicate skill level and are arranged in order from easiest to most challenging.

Confident Beginner:  Must be comfortable rotary cutting straight-grain strips and machine piecing strip units. Confident Beginner patterns are based on simple bias squares and side-by-sides. These patterns are a good introduction to bias strip piecing.

Intermediate:  Must be comfortable with bias strip piecing and machine piecing. Intermediate patterns include striped squares and striped triangles. You are ready for these patterns if you are comfortable with bias strip piecing. If you are not sure, make a pair of Lost Ships blocks (page 40) to familiarize yourself with the basics.

Skilled:  Must be comfortable with bias strip piecing and machine piecing. These patterns include striped rectangles or on-point construction techniques and require precise sewing and cutting.

Fabric requirements for all patterns are based on 44"-wide fabrics, which may shrink to 41" from selvage to selvage when washed. If the end of the bolt says the fabric is less than 44" wide, buy extra fabric. To estimate how much extra to buy, check the pattern's cutting requirements, find the largest piece you have to cut, and buy at least this much extra width rounded up to the next 1/4-yard increment. If your fabric measures wider than 41" after washing, you be able to cut extra pieces.

All backing-fabric requirements are based on piecing 41"-wide panels of yardage (see "Making a Quilt Backing" on page 93). If you prefer to piece designed backs, have access to oversized muslin, or prefer other methods of making backings, feel free to disregard the yardage requirements given in the patterns.

In patterns that call for fat quarters, it is assumed that the fat quarter measures no less than 17" x 21" after washing. If your fat quarters shrink too much, you may want to switch to 1/4- or 3/8-yard pieces, depending on the dimensions of the pieces you need to cut.

Some of the scrappy patterns have odd-size fabric requirements, such as 6" x 17". These are given only as a guide. Please note that these pieces will be cut into smaller pieces. You may have fabric in your stash, of a different shape and size than is called for in the materials list, that will yield the needed pieces just as well.

After the initial cutting directions, most patterns provide further instructions for cutting strips, in the form of easy-to-read charts. Unless instructed otherwise, set aside unused corner triangles for a pieced back or another project.

Keep the following points in mind while working with the patterns:

◆ Sew with an accurate 1/4"-wide seam allowance. As with all machine piecing, you will run into problems if your seam allowance is inaccurate. See "Sewing with an Accurate Seam Allowance" on page 10.

◆ Tape or glue a small swatch of fabric next to each set of cutting directions to avoid confusion. Do the same with each Bias Strip Cutting Chart.

◆ Do not cut the corner triangles into bias strips unless directed to do so. Sometimes they are used for other purposes in the pattern.

◆ Be sure the fabric print faces the correct direction, either right side up or right side down, as specified in the instructions.

◆ Press all seam allowances as shown by the arrows or "ears" in the illustrations, or as instructed in the text. Pressing directions are important to the success of the patterns and are clearly specified every step of the way. If you follow the pressing directions, the seams, including diagonal ones, will butt at intersections, with few exceptions.

◆ Add borders as instructed in each pattern. Most of the patterns use straight-cut, or plain, borders. Sew the border strips end to end to make one long border strip. Measure and cut borders from this single long strip as needed. If you prefer unpieced borders or another method, adjust the border-fabric requirements to suit your technique.

◆ Patterns beginning on page 81 use the on-point construction techniques described on page 24. Be sure to read the pattern instructions carefully and to use the correct ruler indicated in each step. You will use a standard rotary ruler and the Bias Stripper ruler for slightly different tasks.

◆ When all else fails, read the instructions!

Bob's Lost Ships

Color Photo on page 28 ◆ Finished Quilt Size: 51" x 51" ◆ Finished Block Size: 6" x 6"

The blocks in this quilt are made in pairs from different dark and light prints. It's a great opportunity to use up the fabrics in your stash. As you can see from the three photos shown on pages 28–29, this quilt can look quite different depending on the fabrics used. For "Bob's Lost Ships," I used dark and light blue, purple, and green prints.

Hint: *if you use the same background print for all the blocks, a secondary ship will be reflected "in the water" below each ship. This effect is muted when each background print is different.*

Materials: 44"-wide fabric

21 dark prints, each 7" x 18"

21 light prints, each 7" x 18"

¾ yd. blue print

4 different light squares, each 10" x 10", for side-setting triangles

2 different light squares, each 5½" x 5½", for corner-setting triangles

⅜ yd. for binding

3¼ yds. for backing

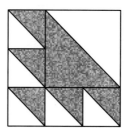

Lost Ships

▨ Assorted darks

☐ Assorted lights

Cutting

All measurements include ¼"-wide seam allowances.

From *each* dark and light print, cut:

1 piece, 6" x 16½", for bias strips

From the blue print, cut:

5 strips, each 4½" x 41"

From the fabric for binding, cut:

5 strips, each 2" x 41"

Piecing a Pair of Blocks

Press seam allowances in the direction of the arrows unless otherwise instructed.

1. Pair a 6" x 16½" dark piece with a matching light piece, right sides up. Using the Bias Stripper, cut 3 sets of full bias strips from the layered fabrics at the 2¾" mark. Reserve the 2 dark and 2 light triangles.

2. Sew the bias strips into Strip Unit I. Cut 10 bias squares, each 2½" x 2½".

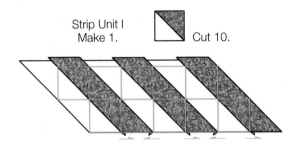

Strip Unit I
Make 1.   Cut 10.

3. Aligning the bias edges, sew each dark triangle to a light triangle. Cut a 4½" bias square from each dark-light unit.

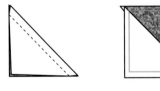

4. Assemble 2 Lost Ships blocks as shown.

Make 2.

5. Repeat steps 1–4 to make 20 more pairs of Lost Ships blocks. You will have a total of 42 blocks.

Assembling and Finishing the Quilt Top

1. Cut each 10" light square twice diagonally to make 16 side-setting triangles. Arrange the side-setting triangles and 41 Lost Ships blocks in diagonal rows. (You will have 1 block left over.) Sew the blocks together, pressing the seams in opposite directions from row to row so the seams will butt. Join the rows.

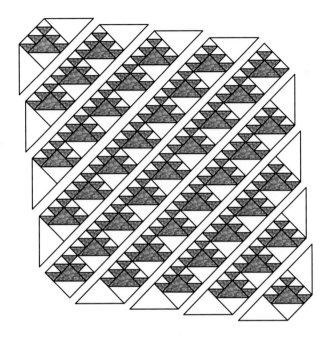

2. Cut each 5½" light square once diagonally. Sew 1 triangle to each corner of the quilt. Trim the quilt top to ¼" from the block corners.

3. Referring to "Plain Borders" on page 91, measure the quilt top, cut the blue strips to size, and then sew the strips to the quilt top.

4. Referring to "Quilt Finishing" on pages 91–96, layer the completed quilt top with batting and backing; baste. Quilt as desired. Bind the edges of the quilt. Add a label.

▨ Assorted darks   ☐ Assorted lights

NEXT DOOR NEIGHBOR

Color Photo on Page 33 ◆ Finished Quilt Size: 54½" x 62½" ◆ Finished Block Size: 8" x 8"

*T*his quilt is built two blocks at a time in fifteen different color combinations. Each color combination consists of one medium and one dark print and a coordinating light print. You will have two blocks in each color combination in which the positions of the medium and dark colors are reversed. As you can see in the three quilts shown on pages 32–33, you can use color and value to achieve very different looks. Instructions are given for the quilt shown, which has fifteen pairs of blocks.

Materials: 44"-wide fabric

1 piece *each* of 15 medium prints, each 8" x 20"

1 piece *each* of 15 dark prints, each 8" x 20"

1 piece *each* of 15 light prints, each 10" x 21"

½ yd. light print for inner border

1⅛ yds. multicolored print for outer border

½ yd. for binding

4 yds. for backing

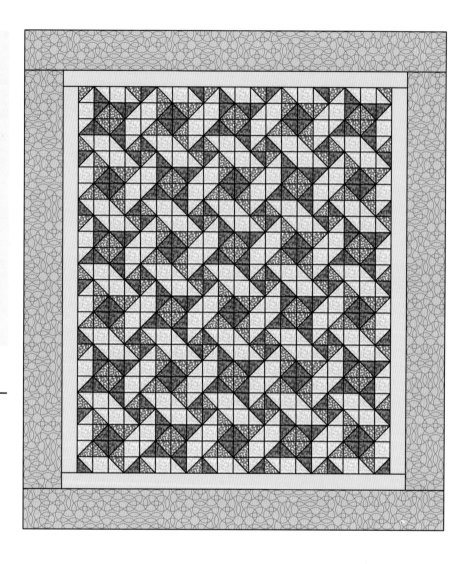

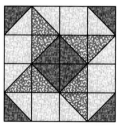

Block A

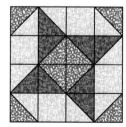

Block B

 Mediums

 Darks

 Lights

Cutting

All measurements include ¼"-wide seam allowances.

From *each* of the 15 medium prints, cut:
3 squares, each 6" x 6", for corner bias strip units

From *each* of the 15 dark prints, cut:
3 squares, each 6" x 6", for corner bias strip units

From *each* of the 15 light prints, cut:
3 squares, each 6" x 6", for corner bias strip units
8 squares, each 2½" x 2½", for blocks

From the light print for the inner border, cut:
5 strips, each 2½" x 41"

From the multicolored print for the outer border, cut:
6 strips, each 5½" x 41"

From the fabric for binding, cut:
6 strips, each 2" x 41"

Piecing a Pair of Blocks

Press seam allowances in the direction of the arrows unless otherwise instructed.

1. Choose three 6" squares, one each from the medium, dark, and light prints. Cut the squares once diagonally to make triangles. Using the Bias Stripper, cut the triangles into corner bias strips at the 2¾" mark.

2¾"

2. Sew pairs of corner bias strips together on the long edges in the following combinations.

      3 pairs of medium and dark
      3 pairs of medium and light
      3 pairs of dark and light

Sew the pairs into strip units as shown. From each strip unit, cut a total of 8 bias squares, each 2½" x 2½". Half the bias squares will be pressed in one direction and half in the other. Stack the squares by color and pressing direction.

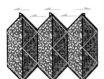 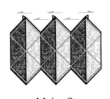

Make 3. 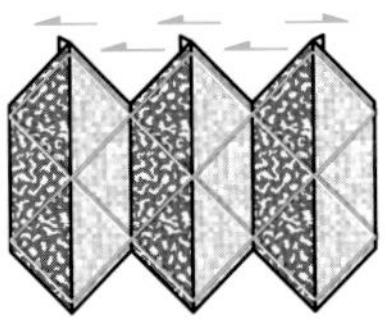   Make 3.   Make 3.

3. Assemble 1 Block A and 1 Block B as shown. Arrange the bias squares according to both color and pressing direction so that the diagonal seams will butt.

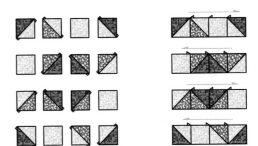

Block A
Make 1.

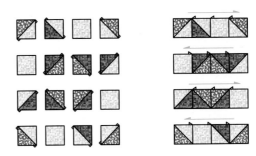

Block B
Make 1.

4. Repeat steps 1–3 to make 14 more pairs of blocks.

Mediums   Darks   Lights

Assembling and Finishing the Quilt Top

1. Arrange the 30 blocks into 6 rows of 5 blocks each. Rotate the blocks so the final 3 seam allowances face up in the A blocks and down in the B blocks. Sew the blocks into rows, pressing the seams in opposite directions from row to row. Join the rows.

2. Referring to "Plain Borders" on page 91, measure the quilt top, cut the light border strips to size, and sew the strips to the quilt top. Repeat for the multi-colored outer border.

3. Referring to "Quilt Finishing" on pages 91–96, layer the completed quilt top with batting and backing; baste. Quilt as desired. Bind the edges of the quilt. Add a label.

| A | B | A | B | A |

| B | A | B | A | B |

| A | B | A | B | A |

| B | A | B | A | B |

| A | B | A | B | A |

| B | A | B | A | B |

Mediums   Darks   Lights

APPLE ORCHARD

Color Photo on Page 29 ◆ Finished Quilt Size: 56⅝" x 56⅝" ◆ Finished Block Size: 12" x 12"

*A*pples are the theme in this cheerful summer quilt. While there may seem to be lots of triangles, remember that they are cut as bias squares, making the chore as light as a summer breeze. Your trees can be peach trees, orange trees, or Christmas trees. Find a theme print to suit your tastes, and collect other prints to match.

Materials: 44"-wide fabric

1 fat quarter *each* of 4 dark green prints

1 fat quarter *each* of 4 medium green prints

1 fat quarter brown print

⅜ yd. red print

⅞ yd. light print

1¼ yds. light blue floral print

⅝ yd. dark blue print

1 yd. apple print

½ yd. for binding

3¾ yds. for backing

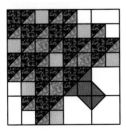

Apple Tree Block

- ▨ Dark greens
- ▨ Medium greens
- ▨ Brown
- ▨ Red
- ☐ Light
- ▫ Light blue
- ▨ Dark blue
- ▨ Apple print

Cutting

All measurements include ¼"-wide seam allowances.

From *each* dark green print, cut:
1 piece, 9½" x 18½", for Strip Unit I
11 squares, each 2" x 2", for blocks. Cut 1 additional
2" square from leftover fabric for a total of 45
squares.

From *each* medium green print, cut:
1 piece, 9½" x 18½", for Strip Unit I
4 squares, each 2" x 2", for blocks (you will have 1
extra square)

From the brown print, cut:
1 square, 9½" x 9½", for Strip Unit II
20 squares, each 2" x 2", for blocks

From the red print, cut:
2 strips, each 2" x 41"; crosscut into 35 squares,
each 2" x 2", for blocks
5 strips, each 1¼" x 41", for inner border

From the light print, cut:
2 strips, each 3½" x 41"; crosscut into
15 squares, each 3½" x 3½", for blocks
10 rectangles, each 3½" x 2", for blocks
1 strip, 2" x 41"; crosscut into 20 squares, each
2" x 2", for blocks
2 strips, each 1¼" x 41", for Strip Unit III
6 strips, each 2" x 41", for Strip Unit IV

From the light blue floral print, cut:
1 square, 23" x 23", for side-setting triangles
2 squares, each 14" x 14", for corner-setting triangles

From the dark blue print, cut:
12 strips, each 1¼" x 41", for Strip Unit IV

From the apple print, cut:
1 strip, 2" x 41", for Strip Unit III
6 strips, each 4½" x 41", for outer border

From the fabric for binding, cut:
6 strips, each 2" x 41"

Bias Strip Cutting Chart

FABRIC	NO. OF 9½" x 18½" PIECES	CUTTING MARK	TOTAL NO. FULL BIAS STRIPS	STRIP UNIT
Dark green	4	2¼"	12	I
Medium green	4	2¼"	12	I

Using the Bias Stripper, cut the number of full bias strips indicated in the chart. If you are right-handed, cut all fabrics face up. If you are left-handed, cut all fabrics face down. Reserve 4 dark green and 2 medium green corner triangles to use during quilt construction.

Piecing the Blocks

Press seam allowances in the direction of the arrows unless otherwise instructed.

1. Using the Bias Stripper, cut 2 dark green and 2 medium green reserved corner triangles into bias strips at the 2¼" mark. Using the dark and medium green full bias strips cut previously and the corner bias strips, assemble 2 of Strip Unit I. Cut a total of 110 bias squares, each 2" x 2".

Strip Unit I
Make 2.

 Cut 110.

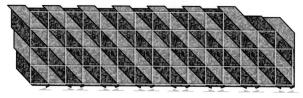

For each strip unit, use:
■ 6 full bias strips at 2¼" mark and corner bias strips
■ 6 full bias strips at 2¼" mark and corner bias strips

2. Cut the 9½" brown square once diagonally to make 2 triangles. Pair each brown triangle with the 2 remaining dark green reserved triangles, aligning the bias edges and 1 set of points. Using the Bias Stripper, cut each triangle pair into 1 set of corner bias strips at the 2¼" mark. Use the corner bias strips to assemble Strip Unit II. Cut 10 bias squares, each 2" x 2".

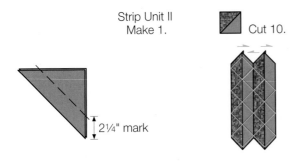

Strip Unit II
Make 1.

Cut 10.

2¼" mark

3. Assemble the number of pieced squares (A–J) indicated below.

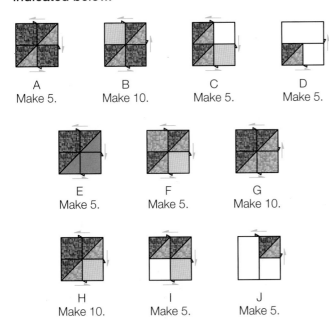

A
Make 5.

B
Make 10.

C
Make 5.

D
Make 5.

E
Make 5.

F
Make 5.

G
Make 10.

H
Make 10.

I
Make 5.

J
Make 5.

4. Using a white or yellow pencil so the line will show, draw a line from corner to corner on the wrong side of the 15 remaining 2" brown squares. With right sides together, place a brown square on a corner of each 3½" light square and pin in place. Stitch on the pencil line. Trim ¼" from the seam. Press the seam allowance toward the light square in 10 blocks and toward the brown triangle in 5 blocks.

Make 15.

5. Arrange squares A–J and the units from step 4 into rows as shown. Be careful to orient the pieced blocks and the units made in step 4 correctly. Sew the blocks into rows, pressing the seams in opposite directions from row to row. Join the rows to complete an Apple Orchard block. Make 5 blocks.

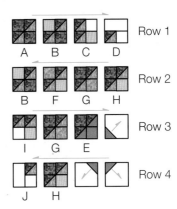

Row 1
A   B   C   D

Row 2
B   F   G   H

Row 3
I   G   E

Row 4
J   H

Assembling and Finishing the Quilt Top

1. Using the 2" x 41" apple print strip and the 2 light 1¼" x 41" strips, make 1 Strip Unit III. Cut 12 segments, each 2" wide.

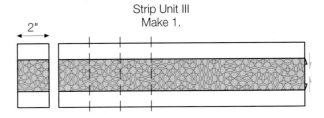

Strip Unit III
Make 1.

2"

2. Using the 1¼" x 41" dark blue strips and the 2" x 41" light strips, make 6 Strip Unit IV. Cut 16 segments, each 12½" wide. Cut 24 segments, each 1¼" wide, from the leftovers. Re-press seam allowances of the 12½"-wide segments toward the light center strip.

Strip Unit IV
Make 6.

 Dark greens   Medium greens   Brown   Red   Light   Light blue   Dark blue   Apple print

3. Assemble the sashing cornerstones as shown.

Make 12.

4. Cut the 23" light blue floral squares twice diagonally to make 4 side-setting triangles.

5. Assemble the blocks, sashing strips, and cornerstones into rows as shown. Press all seam allowances toward the sashing strips.

6. Join the rows, pressing the seam allowances toward the sashing strips. Cut the two 14" light blue floral squares once diagonally to make 4 corner triangles. Sew the triangles to the corners of the quilt top. Trim the quilt top to ¼" from the block corners.

7. Referring to "Plain Borders" on page 91, measure the quilt top, cut the red border strips to size, and then sew the strips to the quilt top. Repeat for the apple print outer border.

8. Referring to "Quilt Finishing" on pages 91–96, layer the completed quilt top with batting and backing; baste. Quilt as desired. Bind the edges of the quilt. Add a label.

 Dark greens   Medium greens   Brown   Red   Light   Light blue   Dark blue   Apple print

Star of Destiny

Color Photo on Page 33 ◈ Finished Quilt Size: 65½" x 65½" ◈ Finished Block Size: 9" x 9"

*T*hese stars sparkle and dance against a black background. The Star of Destiny pattern would be equally at home with warm country colors or pretty pastels. For a different look, try a light background with lots of quilting in the open areas. Don't forget that even though the pattern calls for a pieced border, you can always substitute a large-scale multicolored print that pulls the other prints together.

Materials: 44"-wide fabric

1⅛ yds. red print

1⅛ yds. gold print

¼ yd. *each* of 7 green prints

2⅛ yds. black solid

2 yds. dark multicolored print

½ yd. for binding

4¼ yds. for backing

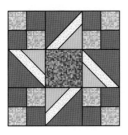

Star of Destiny

▨ Red

☐ Gold

▦ Greens

▧ Black

▨ Dark multicolored

Cutting

From the red print, cut:
   3 pieces, each 12" x 41", for Strip Units I and III

From the gold print, cut:
   3 pieces, each 12" x 41", for Strip Units I and III

From *each* green print, cut:
   1 strip, 2" x 41", for Strip Unit II
   4 squares, each 2½" x 2½", for cornerstones
      (you will have 3 left over)

From the black solid, cut:
   2 pieces, each 12" x 41", for Strip Unit I
   7 strips, each 2" x 41", for Strip Unit II
   10 strips, each 2½" x 41"; crosscut into 40 strips,
      each 2½" x 9½", for sashing
   5 strips, each 1½" x 41", for inner border

From the dark multicolored print, cut:
   2 pieces, each 12" x 41", for Strip Unit III
   2 strips, each 3½" x 41"; crosscut into 20 squares,
      each 3½" x 3½", for block centers and pieced
      border
   6 strips, each 6" x 41", for outer border

From the fabric for binding, cut:
   7 strips, each 2" x 41"

Bias Strip Cutting Chart

FABRIC	NO. OF 12" x 41" PIECES	CUTTING MARK	TOTAL NO. FULL BIAS STRIPS	STRIP UNIT
Red	3	2¾"	24	I, III
Gold	3	1"	44	I, III
Black	2	3¾"	11	I
Dark multicolored	2	3¾"	12	III

Using the Bias Stripper, cut the number of full bias strips indicated in the chart. If you are right-handed, cut all fabrics face up. If you are left-handed, cut all fabrics face down.

Piecing the Blocks

   Press seam allowances in the direction of the arrows unless otherwise instructed.

1. Sew a gold bias strip to the right side of 11 red bias strips and to each of the 11 black solid bias strips. Join the red and black units in pairs, sewing each gold-black pair to the right of each red-gold pair.

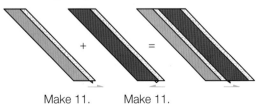

Make 11.   Make 11.

2. Sew the 11 units together to make 1 large Strip Unit I as shown. Sew the remaining red bias strip to the right side of the strip unit. Cut 64 striped squares, each 3½" x 3½".

Strip Unit I
Make 1.   Cut 64.

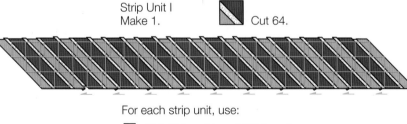

For each strip unit, use:
   ▢ 12 full bias strips at 2¾" mark
   ▢ 22 full bias strips at 1" mark
   ■ 11 full bias strips at 3¾" mark

 Red   Gold   Greens    Black   Dark multicolored

3. Assemble 7 Strip Unit II. Cut a total of 128 segments, each 2" wide.

Strip Unit II
Make 7.

2"

4. Sew 2 segments together to make a four-patch unit. Make 64 units.

Make 64.

5. Assemble 16 Star of Destiny blocks as shown.

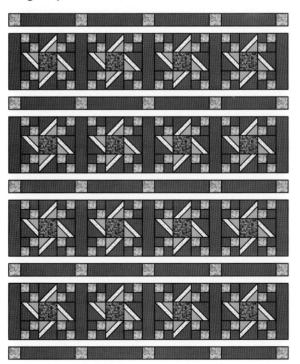

Make 16.

Assembling and Finishing the Quilt Top

1. Arrange the blocks, sashing strips, and green cornerstones into rows as shown. Sew the units into rows, pressing the seam allowances toward the sashing strips. Join the rows.

2. Referring to "Plain Borders" on page 91, measure the quilt top, cut the black solid strips to size, and then sew the strips to the quilt top.

3. Assemble 2 Strip Unit III. Press one strip unit as indicated by the arrows at the top of the illustration and the other as indicated at the bottom. Cut 32 striped squares, each 3½" x 3½", from each strip unit, for a total of 64.

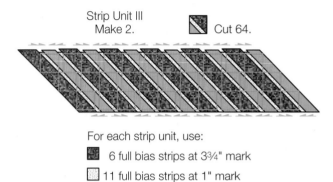

Strip Unit III
Make 2.   Cut 64.

For each strip unit, use:

6 full bias strips at 3¾" mark

11 full bias strips at 1" mark

6 full bias strips at 2¾" mark

4. Sew a striped square that is pressed toward the red print to the right side of each striped square pressed toward the multicolored print.

Make 32 pairs.

5. Join 8 pairs to make a border as shown. Make 4 pieced borders.

Make 4 borders.

6. Sew a pieced border to opposite sides of the quilt top, with the red triangles toward the inner border. Press the seam allowances toward the inner border. Sew a 3½" multicolored square to each end of the 2 remaining borders. Press the seam allowances toward the squares. Sew the borders to the top and bottom edges of the quilt top and press the seam allowances toward the inner border.

7. Referring to "Plain Borders" on page 91, measure the quilt top, cut the multicolored border strips to size, and then sew the strips to the quilt top.

8. Referring to "Quilt Finishing" on pages 91–96, layer the completed quilt top with batting and backing; baste. Quilt as desired. Bind the edges of the quilt. Add a label.

 Red   Gold   Greens   Black   Dark multicolored

SWEET GARDENS IN THE STARS

Color Photo on Page 36 ◆ Finished Quilt Size: 68¹/₈" x 85¹/₈" ◆ Finished Block Size: 12" x 12"

*D*epending on whether you set the blocks straight or on point, this quilt can look very different, as shown in the photos on pages 36–37. The directions that follow are for the eighteen-block quilt, set on point. If you wish to make the sixteen-block straight-set version, make two fewer blocks and eliminate the 19" small-scale green floral squares.

Materials: 44-wide fabric

1³/₄ yds. purple plaid

1¹/₈ yds. pink print

1³/₈ yds. purple-and-blue print

2¹/₂ yds. small-scale green floral

1¹/₈ yds. light purple print

³/₈ yd. large-scale green floral

³/₄ yd. purple-and-pink print

1³/₈ yds. large-scale purple floral

⁵/₈ yd. for binding

5³/₈ yds. for backing

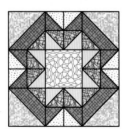

Sweet Garden

■ Purple plaid

□ Pink

■ Purple-and-blue

□ Small-scale green floral

□ Light purple

■ Large-scale green floral

■ Purple-and-pink

■ Large-scale purple floral

Cutting

All measurements include ¼"-wide seam allowances.

From the purple plaid, cut:
    5 pieces, each 11" x 39", for Strip Units I and II
From the pink print, cut:
    1 piece, 11" x 39", for Strip Unit III
    1 piece, 11" x 41"; crosscut into
        1 piece, 11" x 25", for Strip Unit III
        1 square, 11" x 11", for Strip Unit III
    7 strips, each 1½" x 41", for inner border
From the purple-and-blue print, cut:
    4 pieces, each 11" x 39", for Strip Units I and III
From the small-scale green floral, cut:
    4 pieces, each 11" x 39", for Strip Unit I
    3 squares, each 19" x 19", for side-setting triangles
        and corner-setting triangles

From the light purple print, cut:
    1 piece, 11" x 39", for Strip Unit II
    2 pieces, each 11" x 41"; crosscut into 4 squares,
        each 11" x 11", for Strip Unit II
From the large-scale green floral, cut:
    2 strips, each 4½" x 41"; crosscut into 18 squares,
        each 4½" x 4½", for block centers
From the purple-and-pink print, cut:
    7 strips, each 2⅞" x 41", for middle border
From the large-scale purple floral, cut:
    8 strips, each 5½" x 41", for outer border
From the fabric for binding, cut:
    8 strips, each 2" x 41"

Bias Strip Cutting Chart

FABRIC	NO. OF PIECES	SIZE	CUTTING MARK	TOTAL NO. FULL BIAS STRIPS	STRIP UNIT
Purple plaid	5	11" x 39"	2"	36	I
			2¾"	8	II
Pink	1	11" x 39"	2¾"	12	III
	1	11" x 25"			
Purple-and-blue	4	11" x 39"	2¾"	32	I, III
Small-scale green floral	4	11" x 39"	4¾"	18	I
Light purple	1	11" x 39"	2¾"	8	II

Using the Bias Stripper, cut the number of full bias strips indicated in the chart. If you are right-handed, cut all fabrics face up. If you are left-handed, cut all fabrics face down. Reserve 9 purple plaid, 4 pink, 6 purple-and-blue, and 1 light purple corner triangle to use during quilt construction.

Piecing the Blocks

Press seam allowances in the direction of the arrows unless otherwise instructed.

1. Assemble 2 Strip Unit I. Press one strip unit as indicated by the arrows at the top of the illustration and the other as indicated at the bottom. Cut 36 striped squares, each 4½" x 4½", from each strip unit for a total of 72.

Strip Unit I
Make 2.

 Cut 72.

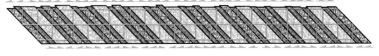

For each strip unit, use:

    9 full bias strips at 4¾" mark

    18 full bias strips at 2" mark

    10 full bias strips at 2¾" mark

2. Cut the 11" light purple squares once diagonally to make 8 triangles. Add the reserved light purple triangle to the stack. With right sides together, pair each of the 9 reserved purple plaid triangles with a light purple triangle. Align the bias edges and 1 set of points. Using the Bias Stripper, cut each triangle pair twice at the 2¾" mark. Discard the small leftover triangles.

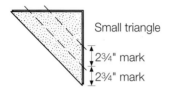

Small triangle

2¾" mark
2¾" mark

3. Using the corner bias strips cut above and the full bias strips cut previously, assemble 1 of each type of Strip Unit II. Cut a total of 144 bias squares, each 2½" x 2½". Stack the square by pressing direction: 72 will be pressed toward the purple plaid and 72 toward the light purple print. If necessary, adjust the pressing on some of the bias squares.

Strip Unit II
Make 1 of each.

 Cut 144.

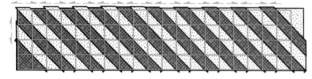

Use:

8 full bias strips at 2¾" mark and corner bias strips

8 full bias strips at 2¾" mark and corner bias strips

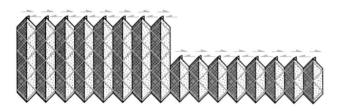

4. Cut the 11" pink square once diagonally to make 2 triangles. Add the reserved pink triangles. With right sides together, pair each pink triangle with one of the reserved purple-and-blue triangles. Align the bias edges and 1 set of points. Using the Bias Stripper, cut each triangle pair twice at the 2¾" mark.

5. Using the assorted pink and purple-and-blue full and corner bias strips, assemble 1 of each type of Strip Unit III. Cut a total of 144 bias squares, each 2½" x 2½". Stack the squares by pressing direction: 72 will be pressed toward the pink and 72 toward the purple–and–blue print. If necessary, adjust the pressing on some of the bias squares.

Strip Unit III
Make 1 of each.

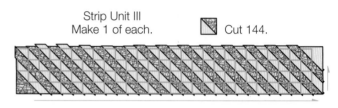 Cut 144.

Use:

☐ 12 full bias strips at 2¾" mark and corner bias strips

▨ 12 full bias strips at 2¾" mark and corner bias strips

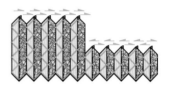

6. Sew the plaid/light purple bias squares together and the pink/purple-blue bias squares into pairs as shown. Note the different pressing arrangements. Sew the pairs together to make 2 types of four-patch units with different seam allowance directions. Make 36 of each type of four-patch unit.

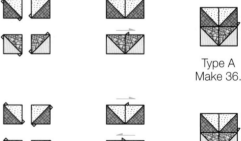

Type A
Make 36.

Type B
Make 36.

7. Assemble 18 Sweet Garden blocks as shown. Note the pressing direction for each unit.

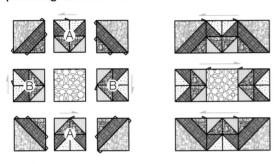

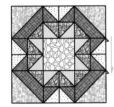

Make 18.

Assembling and Finishing the Quilt Top

1. Cut each 19" small-scale green floral square twice diagonally to make 12 side-setting triangles. Set aside 2 of the triangles to use for corner-setting triangles. Arrange the blocks and the side-setting triangles in diagonal rows, alternating the direction of the final seams from block to block so they will butt when joined. Sew the blocks together. Press the seam allowances in opposite directions from row to row. Join the rows.

2. Cut the 2 reserved small-scale green floral triangles once diagonally to make 4 triangles. Sew them to the corners of the quilt top. Trim the edge of the quilt top to ¼" from the block points.

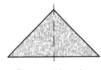

Corner triangles

3. Referring to "Plain Borders" on page 91, measure the quilt top, cut the pink inner-border strips to size, and then sew the strips to the quilt top. Repeat for the purple-and-pink middle border and the purple floral outer border.

4. Referring to "Quilt Finishing" on pages 91–96, layer the completed quilt top with batting and backing; baste. Quilt as desired. Bind the edges of the quilt. Add a label.

 Purple plaid
 Pink
 Purple-and-blue
 Small-scale green floral
 Light purple
 Large-scale green floral
 Purple-and-pink
 Large-scale purple floral

SLEIGHT OF HAND

Color Photo on Page 38 ◆ Finished Quilt Size: 24½" x 24½" ◆ Finished Block Size: 9" x 9"

I've always loved the Card Tricks block. I began playing with the design, adding a few lines here and there, and voilà, with a little "sleight of hand," I came up with this interlocking design. As quick and easy as the little quilt is to make (I made my quilt top in a few hours), it would be fun to repeat the groups of four blocks to make bigger quilts. You could achieve many different looks by varying your fabric choices.

Materials: 44"-wide fabric

⅜ yd. red print

⅜ yd. black floral print

1 yd. light print

¼ yd. for binding

⅞ yd. backing

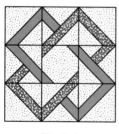

Block A

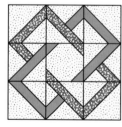

Block B

Red

Black floral

Light

Cutting

From the red print, cut:
1 piece, 9" x 26¼", for Strip Units I and II
1 square, 9" x 9", for Strip Unit VI
8 squares, each 1½" x 1½", for block centers

From the black floral print, cut:
1 piece, 9" x 26¼", for Strip Units III and IV
1 square, 9" x 9", for Strip Unit V
8 squares, each 1½" x 1½", for block centers

From the light print, cut:
2 pieces, each 9" x 41", for Strip Units I, II, III, and IV
1 piece, 9" x 24", for Strip Units I and III
1 square, 9" x 9", for Strip Unit VI
4 squares, each 3½" x 3½", for block centers
2 strips, each 2" x 41", for inner borders

From the fabric for binding, cut:
3 strips, each 2" x 41"

Bias Strip Cutting Chart

FABRIC	NO. OF PIECES	SIZE	CUTTING MARK	TOTAL NO. FULL BIAS STRIPS	STRIP UNIT
Red print	1	9" x 26¼"	1"	6	I, II
			2¾"	2	I
Black floral	1	9" x 26¼"	1"	6	III, IV
			2¾"	2	III
Light print	2	9" x 41"	2¾"	10	I, II, III, IV
			3¾"	4	II, IV
			4"	2	I, III
	1	9" x 24"	3"	4	I, III

Using the Bias Stripper, cut the number of full bias strips indicated in the chart. If you are right-handed, cut all fabrics face up. If you are left-handed, cut all fabrics face down. Reserve all leftover corner triangles to use during quilt construction.

Piecing the Blocks

Press seam allowances in the direction of the arrows unless otherwise instructed. Be careful to position the strips correctly when assembling the strip units.

1. Assemble 1 Strip Unit I. Draw a chalk line through the center of the wide red strips. Align the 1⅜" mark on the short side of the Bias Stripper with the seam line. See page 18 for directions on marking the center of these strips. Referring to the illustration, cut 4 center-stripe squares (A) and 4 regular-stripe squares (B), each 3⅞" x 3⅞".

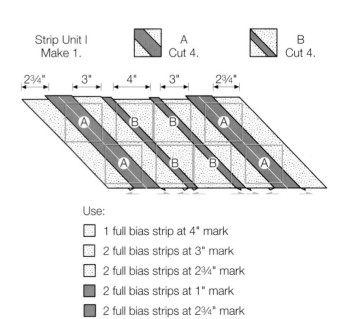

Strip Unit I
Make 1.

A
Cut 4.

B
Cut 4.

Use:
▢ 1 full bias strip at 4" mark
▢ 2 full bias strips at 3" mark
▢ 2 full bias strips at 2¾" mark
▨ 2 full bias strips at 1" mark
▨ 2 full bias strips at 2¾" mark

 Red   Black floral   Light

2. Assemble 1 Strip Unit II. Cut 8 regular-stripe squares, each 3½" x 3½". Be careful to place the ruler's diagonal line on the seam of the 3¾"-wide strip.

Strip Unit II
Make 1.   Cut 8.

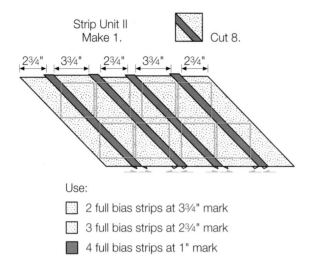

Use:

☐ 2 full bias strips at 3¾" mark

☐ 3 full bias strips at 2¾" mark

■ 4 full bias strips at 1" mark

3. Assemble 1 Strip Unit III. Draw a line through the center of the wide black floral strips as you did for Strip Unit I. Referring to the illustration, cut 4 center-stripe squares (A) and 4 regular-stripe squares (B), each 3⅞" x 3⅞".

Strip Unit III
Make 1.   A Cut 4.   B Cut 4.

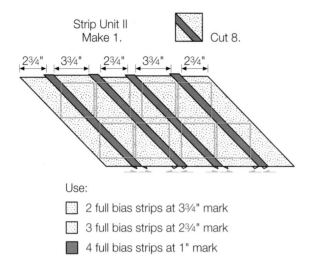

Use:

☐ 1 full bias strip at 4" mark

☐ 2 full bias strips at 3" mark

☐ 2 full bias strips at 2¾" mark

▨ 2 full bias strips at 1" mark

▨ 2 full bias strips at 2¾" mark

4. Assemble 1 Strip Unit IV. Cut 8 regular-stripe squares, each 3½" x 3½". Be careful to place the ruler's diagonal line on the seam of the 3¾"-wide strip.

Strip Unit IV
Make 1.   Cut 8.

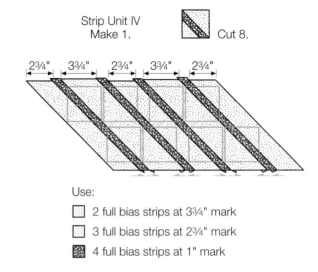

Use:

☐ 2 full bias strips at 3¾" mark

☐ 3 full bias strips at 2¾" mark

▨ 4 full bias strips at 1" mark

5. Cut once diagonally all the 3⅞" striped squares from Strip Units I and III as shown. Do not cut the 3½" striped squares from Strip Units II and IV.

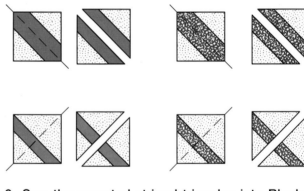

6. Sew the assorted striped triangles into Block A units and Block B units as shown.

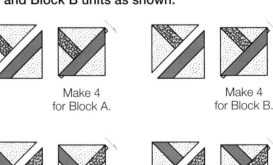

Make 4
for Block A.

Make 4
for Block B.

Make 4
for Block A.

Make 4
for Block B.

 Red   Black floral   ☐ Light

7. Draw a line from corner to corner on the wrong side of each 1½" red and black floral square. Place a red square on the upper right corner of a 3½" light print square, right sides together. Pin the square in place and stitch on the line. Trim ¼" from the stitching line and press the triangle toward the corner. Sew a second red square to the opposite corner in the same manner. Sew a black square to the remaining 2 corners to complete a block center.

Make 4.

8. Assemble 2 Block A and 2 Block B, orienting the units as shown.

Block A
Make 2.

Block B
Make 2.

Assembling and Finishing the Quilt Top

1. Arrange the blocks as shown. Join the blocks. Press the final seam in either direction.

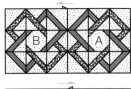
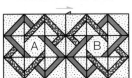
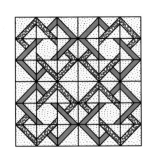

2. Referring to "Plain Borders" on page 91, measure the quilt top, cut the light print border strips to size, and then sew them to the quilt top.

3. Cut the 9" black floral square once diagonally to make 2 triangles. Add the reserved 9" black floral corner triangles to the stack. Pair each of the 4 reserved light corner triangles with a black floral triangle, placing right sides together. Align the bias edges and 1 set of points. Using the Bias Stripper, cut each triangle pair twice at the 2¼" mark.

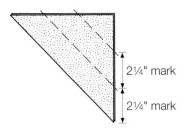

2¼" mark

2¼" mark

4. Join the pairs of corner bias strips on their long edges and assemble into Strip Unit V as shown. Cut 28 bias squares, each 2" x 2". Stack the squares according to pressing direction: 14 will be pressed toward the black floral and 14 toward the light print.

Strip Unit V
Make 1.

 Cut 28.

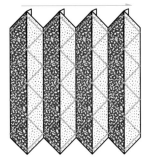

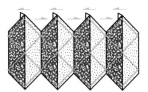

 Red   Black floral   Light

5. Cut the 9" light square once diagonally to make 2 triangles. Add the last 2 reserved light triangles to the stack. Repeat step 3 with the 9" red square, reserved 9" red triangles, and 3 remaining 9" light triangles. Assemble Strip Unit VI as shown and cut 32 bias squares, each 2" x 2". Stack the squares according to pressing direction: 16 will be pressed toward the red print and 16 toward the light print.

Strip Unit VI
Make 1.

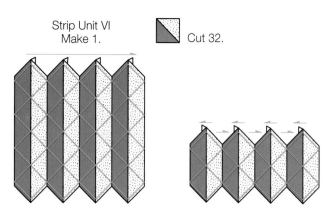

Cut 32.

6. Sew the red bias squares into 16 pairs as shown. Note the pressing direction; you want the diagonal seams to butt when you stitch. Follow the same procedure to sew the black floral bias squares into 12 pairs. You'll use the 4 remaining black floral bias squares later.

Make 16.

Make 12.

7. Sew the bias-square pairs into 4 pieced border strips, alternating black floral and red pairs as shown. Sew a black floral bias square to each end of 2 borders. Note the pressing direction; you want the diagonal seams to butt when you stitch. Press seam allowances toward the right.

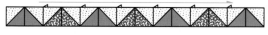

Make 2.

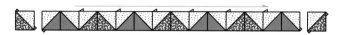

Make 2.

8. Sew short pieced borders to opposite sides of the quilt top, points facing in. Press the seam allowances toward the inner border. Sew the remaining pieced borders to the top and bottom of the quilt top, points facing in. Press the seam allowances toward the inner border.

9. Referring to "Quilt Finishing" on pages 91–96, layer the completed quilt top with batting and backing; baste. Quilt as desired. Bind the edges of the quilt. Add a label.

■ Red   ▨ Black floral   ▯ Light

PANSY PATCH

Color Photo on Page 31 ◈ Finished Quilt Size: 61" x 61" ◈ Finished Block Size: 9" x 9"

My love of gardening shows up frequently in my quilts. My version of this pattern reflects my love of English border gardens, but can't you picture it done in Southwestern prints to mimic cactus flowers? In fact, you can choose prints to make the garden of your choice without getting your hands dirty at all.

This quilt is a bouquet of bias strip-piecing techniques: the side-by-sides for the leaves, the center-stripe square for the stems (my favorite), and the regular-stripe squares for the flower petals. Once you've finished the strip piecing, the block is as easy to assemble as a simple nine patch.

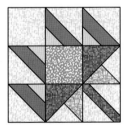

Pansy Patch

- ■ Purple
- □ Gold
- □ Light
- ▨ Pansy print
- ▨ Dark green
- ▨ Medium green
- ▨ Floral

Materials: 44"-wide fabric

1⅛ yds. purple print

⅞ yd. gold print

1⅝ yds. light print

¼ yd. pansy print

¾ yd. dark green print

⅞ yd. medium green print

1¼ yds. floral print

½ yd. for binding

4 yds. for backing

Cutting

All measurements include ¼"-wide seam allowances.

From the purple print, cut:
  2 pieces, each 12" x 41", for Strip Unit I
  5 strips, each 1¾" x 41", for inner border

From the gold print, cut:
  2 pieces, each 12" x 41", for Strip Unit I

From the light print, cut:
  2 pieces, each 12" x 41", for Strip Unit I
  1 piece, 12" x 41", for Strip Unit II
  2 strips, each 3½" x 41"; crosscut into 16 squares,
    each 3½" x 3½", for blocks
  4 strips, each 2½" x 41"; crosscut into 16 strips,
    each 2½" x 9½", for sashing strips

From the pansy print, cut:
  2 strips, each 3½" x 41"; crosscut into 16 squares,
    each 3½" x 3½", for blocks

From the dark green print, cut:
  1 piece, 12" x 41"; crosscut into
    1 piece, 12" x 22¼", for Strip Unit II
    25 squares, each 2½" x 2½", for sashing squares
  2 strips, each 3⅞" x 41"; crosscut into 16 squares,
    each 3⅞" x 3⅞", for blocks

From the medium green print, cut:
  1 strip, 12" x 41"; crosscut into 3 squares, each
    12" x 12", for Strip Unit III
  6 strips, each 2½" x 41"; crosscut into 24 strips,
    each 2½" x 9½", for sashing strips

From the floral print, cut:
  6 strips, each 6½" x 41", for outer border

From the fabric for binding, cut:
  7 strips, each 2" x 41"

Bias Strip Cutting Chart

FABRIC	NO. OF PIECES	SIZE	CUTTING MARK	TOTAL NO. FULL BIAS STRIPS	STRIP UNIT
Purple	2	12" x 41"	1½"	22	I
Gold	2	12" x 41"	2¼"	12	I
Light	2	12" x 41"	3¾"	12	I
	1	12" x 41"	3¼"	7	II
Dark green	1	12" x 22¼"	1"	6	II

Using the Bias Stripper, cut the number of full bias strips indicated in the chart. If you are right-handed, cut all fabrics face up. If you are left-handed, cut all fabrics face down. Reserve the 6 leftover light print corner triangles to use during quilt construction.

Piecing the Blocks

Press seam allowances in the direction of the arrows unless otherwise instructed.

1. Assemble 2 Strip Unit I. Cut a total of 64 striped squares, each 3½" x 3½".

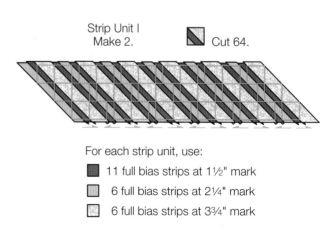

Strip Unit I
Make 2.

Cut 64.

For each strip unit, use:
  ■ 11 full bias strips at 1½" mark
  ▨ 6 full bias strips at 2¼" mark
  □ 6 full bias strips at 3¾" mark

 Purple   Gold   Light   Pansy print   Dark green   Medium green   Floral

2. Assemble 1 Strip Unit II. Draw a chalk line through the center of each dark green bias strip. Align the ½" mark on the short side of the Bias Stripper with the seam line. See page 18 for directions on marking the center of these strips. Cut 16 center-stripe squares, each 3½" x 3½".

Strip Unit II
Make 1.   Cut 16.

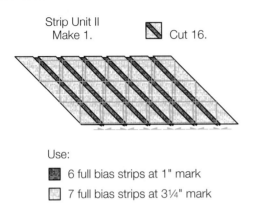

Use:

⬛ 6 full bias strips at 1" mark

⬜ 7 full bias strips at 3¼" mark

3. Cut the 3 medium green 12" squares once diagonally to make 6 triangles. Pair each reserved 12" light corner triangle with a medium green triangle, placing right sides together. Align the bias edges and 1 set of points. Using the Bias Stripper, cut 1 set of bias strips from each pair of triangles at the 4" mark. Join the paired strips along their long bias edges and assemble them into Strip Unit III as shown. Cut 16 bias squares, each 3⅞" x 3⅞".

Strip Unit II
Make 1.   Cut 16.

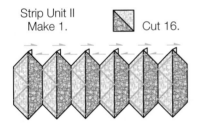

4. Cut each 3⅞" bias square once diagonally to make 32 side-by-sides. Cut the 16 dark green 3⅞" squares once diagonally to make 32 half-square triangles. Sew each dark green triangle to a side-by-side to make 16 Type A and 16 Type B flower sepals.

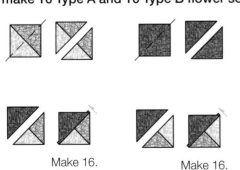

Make 16.   Make 16.
Type A   Type B

5. Assemble 16 Pansy Patch blocks as shown.

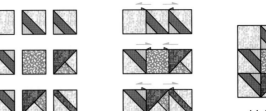

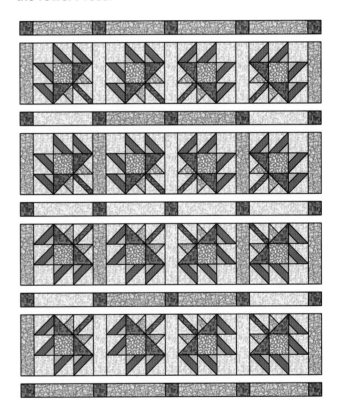

Make 16.

Assembling and Finishing the Quilt Top

1. Arrange the blocks, light sashing strips, light green sashing strips, and dark green sashing squares into rows as shown. Sew the units into rows. Press all seam allowances toward the sashing strips. Join the rows. Press.

2. Referring to "Plain Borders" on page 91, measure the quilt top, cut the purple border strips to size, and then sew the strips to the quilt top. Repeat for the floral outer border.

3. Referring to "Quilt Finishing" on pages 91–96, layer the completed quilt top with batting and backing; baste. Quilt as desired. Bind the edges of the quilt. Add a label.

 Purple   Gold   Light   Pansy print   Dark green   Medium green   Floral

STAR CROSSED

Color Photo on Page 37 ◆ Finished Quilt Size: 58¹/₂" x 82¹/₂" ◆ Finished Block Size: 9" x 9"

It may be difficult at first to figure out how this quilt is put together. The secret is in the pieced sashing strips, which mimic the blocks and create an overlay effect. "Star Crossed" is composed of twenty-four blocks, but the pieced sashing strips make it seem there are thirty-nine. I like to use pieced sashings to make quilts that look more intricate than they really are. A good way to choose fabrics is to begin with one multicolored print for the border and some of the block pieces. Coordinate the rest of your fabrics with this print.

Materials: 44"-wide fabric

1¹/₂ yds. brown print

2¹/₂ yds. dark purple print

1¹/₈ yds. dark green print

³/₈ yd. light purple print

¹/₂ yd. medium green print

2³/₄ yds. light print

⁷/₈ yd. black print

¹/₂ yd. for binding

5¹/₈ yds. for backing

Star Crossed

Brown		Medium green
Dark purple		Light
Dark green		Black
Light purple		

Cutting *All measurements include ¼"-wide seam allowances.*

From the brown print, cut:
  4 pieces, each 12" x 41", for Strip Unit I
From the dark purple print, cut:
  4 pieces, each 9" x 41", for Strip Units II, III, and IV
  1 piece, 9" x 41"; crosscut into
    1 piece, 9" x 18½", for Strip Units II, III, and IV
    30 squares, each 2" x 2", for sashing squares
  7 strips, each 5½" x 41", for outer border
From the dark green print, cut:
  3 pieces, each 9" x 41", for Strip Units II, V, and VI
  1 piece, 9" x 41"; crosscut into
    1 piece, 9" x 18½", for Strip Units II, V, and VI
    40 squares, each 2" x 2", for blocks. Cut 8 more
      2" squares from leftovers.
From the light purple print, cut:
  1 piece, 9" x 41"; crosscut into
    1 piece, 9" x 23¼", for Strip Unit V
    30 squares, each 2" x 2", for sashing squares

From the medium green print, cut:
  1 piece, 9" x 41"; crosscut into:
    1 piece, 9" x 32¾", for Strip Unit III
    8 squares, each 2" x 2", for blocks
  2 strips, each 2" x 41"; crosscut into 40 squares,
    each 2" x 2", for blocks
From the light print, cut:
  3 pieces, each 9" x 41", for Strip Units IV and VI
  4 pieces, each 12" x 41", for Strip Unit I
  5 strips, each 3½" x 41"; crosscut into
    22 squares, each 3½" x 3½", for pieced sashing
    16 rectangles, each 3½" x 6½", for pieced sashing
From the black print, cut:
  4 strips, each 3½" x 41"; crosscut into 39 squares,
    each 3½" x 3½", for block centers and sashing
    squares
  6 strips, each 2" x 41", for inner border
From the fabric for binding, cut:
  7 strips, each 2" x 41"

Bias Strip Cutting Chart

FABRIC	NO. OF PIECES	SIZE	CUTTING MARK	TOTAL NO. FULL BIAS STRIPS	STRIP UNIT
Brown	4	12" x 41"	2"	33	I
Dark purple	4	9" x 41"	4"	26	II, III, IV
	1	9" x 18½"			
Dark green	3	9" x 41"	4"	20	II, V, VI
	1	9" x 18½"			
Light purple	1	9" x 23¼"	4"	3	V
Medium green	1	9" x 32¾"	4"	5	III
Light	3	9" x 41"	4"	18	IV, VI
	4	12" x 41"	2¾"	30	I

Using the Bias Stripper, cut the number of full bias strips indicated in the chart. If you are right-handed, cut all fabrics face up. If you are left-handed, cut all fabrics face down. Reserve 4 dark purple, 3 dark green, 2 light purple, 2 medium green, and 3 light 9" leftover corner triangles, as well as 6 light 12" corner triangles, to use during quilt construction.

 Brown   Dark purple   Dark green   Light purple   Medium green   Light   Black

Piecing the Blocks

Press seam allowances in the direction of the arrows unless otherwise instructed.

1. Using the Bias Stripper, cut 1 bias strip at the 2¾" mark from each of the 6 reserved 12" light corner triangles. Assemble 3 Strip Unit I as shown. Sew a light corner bias strip to each end of each strip unit. Draw a chalk line through the center of each dark bias strip. Align the 1" mark on the short side of the Bias Stripper with the seam line. See page 18 for directions on marking the center of these strips. Cut 96 center-stripe squares, each 3½" x 3½".

2¾"

Strip Unit I
Make 3.

Cut 96.

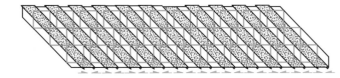

For each strip unit, use:

☐ 10 full bias strips at 2¾" mark and 2 corner bias strips

▨ 11 full bias strips at 2" mark

2. Assemble 1 of each type of Strip Unit II. Sew 2 reserved dark green and 2 dark purple 9" triangles to the strip units as shown. Cut 39 bias squares, each 3⅞" x 3⅞".

Strip Unit II
Make 1 of each.

Cut 39.

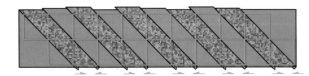

Use:

▨ 5 full bias strips at 4" mark

■ 4 full bias strips at 4" mark and 2 corner triangles

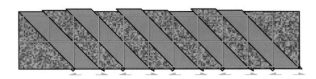

Use:

▨ 4 full bias strips at 4" mark and 2 corner triangles

■ 5 full bias strips at 4" mark

3. Assemble 1 Strip Unit III. Sew 2 reserved medium green 9" corner triangles to the strip unit as shown. Cut 24 bias squares, each 3⅞" x 3⅞".

Strip Unit III
Make 1.

Cut 24.

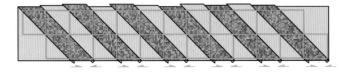

Use:

▨ 6 full bias strips at 4" mark

▨ 5 full bias strips at 4" mark and 2 corner triangles

4. Assemble 1 of each type of Strip Unit IV. Sew 2 reserved light and 2 dark purple 9" corner triangles to the strip units as shown. Cut a total of 48 bias squares, each 3⅞" x 3⅞".

Strip Unit IV
Make 1 of each.

Cut 48.

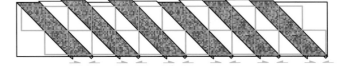

Use:

▨ 6 full bias strips at 4" mark

☐ 5 full bias strips at 4" mark and 2 corner triangles

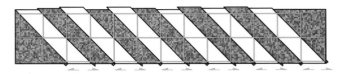

Use:

▨ 5 full bias strips at 4" mark and 2 corner triangles

☐ 6 full bias strips at 4" mark

 Brown   Dark purple   Dark green   Light purple   Medium green   Light ■ Black

5. Cut 24 of the dark green/dark purple bias squares, the 48 dark purple/light bias squares, and the 24 dark purple/medium green bias squares once diagonally to make side-by sides.

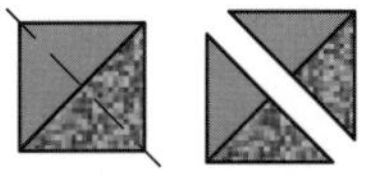

Cut 24 into side-by-sides. 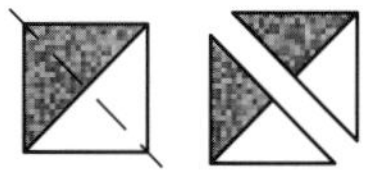   Cut 48 into side-by-sides.

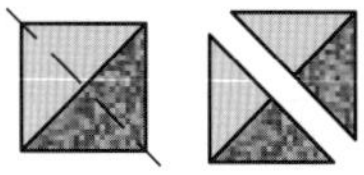

Cut 24 into side-by-sides.

6. Sew a dark purple/light side-by-side to each of the other side-by-sides to make 24 each of 4 units. Press all seam allowances toward the dark purple/light side-by-side.

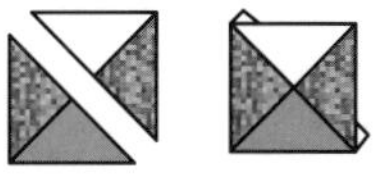

Make 24. 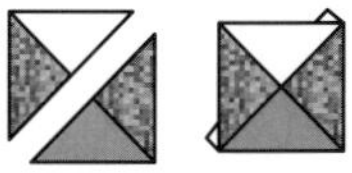   Make 24.

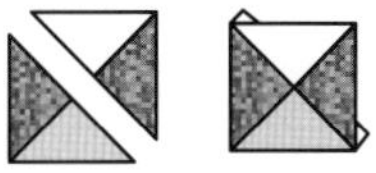

Make 24. 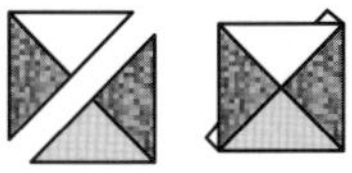   Make 24.

7. Draw a line from corner to corner on the wrong side of each dark green and each medium green 2" square. With right sides together, place a marked 2" dark green square on a 3½" black square as shown. Sew on the line. Trim ¼" beyond the seam. Press the seam allowance toward the triangle. Sew another 2" dark green square and two 2" medium green squares to the corners of the black square as shown. Make 24 block centers.

Make 24.

8. Assemble 24 Star Crossed blocks as shown.

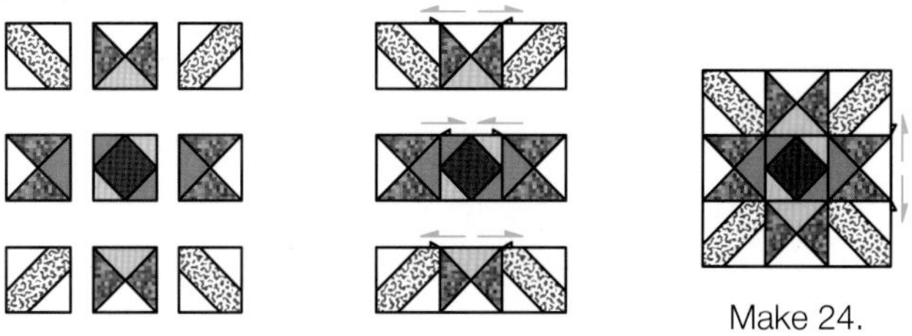

Make 24.

Assembling and Finishing the Quilt Top

1. Assemble 1 Strip Unit V. Sew 2 reserved light purple 9" corner triangles to the sides of the strip unit. Cut 15 bias squares, each 3⅞" x 3⅞".

Strip Unit V
Make 1.   Cut 15.

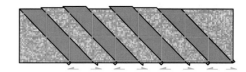

Use:

■ 4 full bias strips at 4" mark

▨ 3 full bias strips at 4" mark and 2 corner triangles

2. Assemble 1 Strip Unit VI. Sew 1 reserved dark green and 1 reserved light 9" corner triangle to the sides of the strip unit. Cut 30 bias squares, each 3⅞" x 3⅞".

Strip Unit VI
Make 1.   Cut 30.

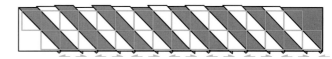

Use:

■ 7 full bias strips at 4" mark and 1 corner triangle

□ 7 full bias strips at 4" mark and 1 corner triangle

 Brown   Dark purple   Dark green   Light purple   Medium green   Light   Black

3. Cut 15 dark purple/dark green bias squares, the 30 dark green/light bias squares, and the 15 dark green/medium purple bias squares once diagonally to make side-by-sides.

Cut 15 into side-by-sides. Cut 30 into side-by-sides.

Cut 15 into side-by-sides.

4. Sew a dark green/light side-by-side to each of the other side-by-sides to make 15 each of 4 units. Press all seam allowances toward the dark green/light side-by-side.

Make 15. Make 15.

Make 15. Make 15.

5. Follow the procedure in step 7 on page 67 to make 15 sashing squares, using 15 black 3½" squares and 30 dark purple and 30 medium purple 2" squares.

Make 15 sashing cornerstones.

6. Arrange the blocks, side-by-side units, sashing cornerstones, 3½" light squares, and 3½" x 6½" light rectangles in rows as shown. Sew the units together and press all seam allowances toward the sashing strips. Join the rows.

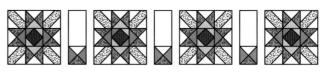

Make 2 end rows (top and bottom rows).

Make 5 sashing rows.

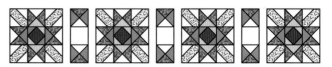

Make 4 center rows.

7. Referring to "Plain Borders" on page 91, measure the quilt top, cut the black print border strips to size, then sew the strips to the quilt top. Repeat for the dark purple outer border.

8. Referring to "Quilt Finishing" on pages 91–96, layer the completed quilt top with batting and backing; baste. Quilt as desired. Bind the edges of the quilt. Add a label.

Brown Dark purple Dark green Light purple Medium green Light Black

DESERT DOGS

Color Photo on Page 30 ◆ Finished Quilt Size: 55¼" x 55¼" ◆ Finished Block Size: 10" x 10"

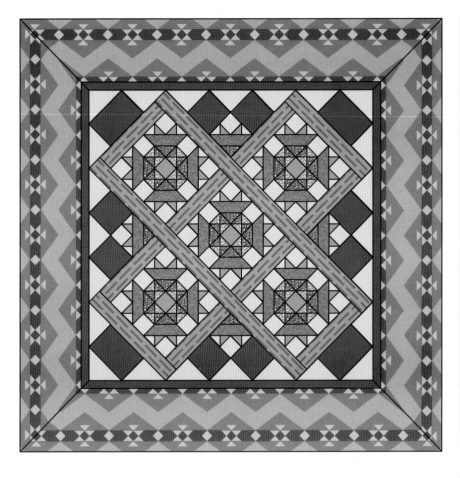

This quilt offers the opportunity to try a couple of bias strip piecing techniques by making both side-by-sides and center-stripe triangles. The five blocks are set on point with pieced side-setting triangles to add dimension to the design. Deb thought mitered corners would look best with her border print, but mitering isn't necessary for all prints— you be the judge.

The key to fabric selection is to choose a multicolored border print first and then find coordinating prints to use in the center of the quilt. The bold southwestern theme of the quilt shown on page 30 is just one possibility. Try a pretty floral for a garden quilt; red, white, and blue for a patriotic theme; or whatever your heart desires.

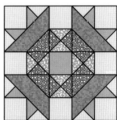

Desert Dogs

▨	Purple
▨	Orange
▨	Black floral
☐	Peach
▨	Teal #1
▬	Teal #2
▨	Black
▨	Border print

Materials: 44"-wide fabric

¾ yd. purple print

⅜ yd. orange print

¾ yd. black floral

⅞ yd. peach solid

⅜ yd. teal print #1

½ yd. teal print #2

½ yd. black print

1¾ yds. border print

½ yd. for binding

3⅝ yds. for backing

Cutting

From the purple print, cut:
    1 piece, 11" x 41", for Strip Unit I
    1 piece, 11" x 16½", for Strip Unit I

From the orange print, cut:
    1 piece, 10" x 21¼", for Strip Unit II
    5 squares, each 2½" x 2½", for blocks

From the black floral print, cut:
    1 piece, 11" x 35¼", for Strip Unit I
    1 square, 11" x 11", for Strip Unit III

From the peach solid, cut:
    1 piece, 10" x 41"; crosscut into
        1 piece, 10" x 21¼", for Strip Unit II
        28 squares, each 2½" x 2½", for blocks
    1 strip, 2½" x 41"; crosscut into 16 squares, each
        2½" x 2½", for blocks
    5 squares, each 7¼" x 7¼", for side-setting triangles
    2 squares, each 5½" x 5½", for pieced corner-setting
        triangles

From teal print #1, cut:
    2 squares, each 11" x 11", for Strip Unit III

From teal print #2, cut:
    6 strips, each 2½" x 41"; crosscut into
        8 strips, each 2½" x 10½", for sashing strips
        2 strips, each 2½" x 38½", for sashing strips
        2 strips, each 2½" x 14½", for sashing strips

From the black print, cut:
    2 strips, each 4½" x 41"; crosscut into
        8 squares, each 4½" x 4½", for pieced side-setting
            triangles
        4 rectangles, each 4½" x 6½", for pieced corner-
            setting triangles
    4 strips, each 1½" x 41", for mitered inner border

**From the border print, cut from the length of
the fabric:**
    4 strips, each 8½" x 57", for mitered outer border

From the fabric for binding, cut:
    6 strips, each 2" x 41"

Bias Strip Cutting Chart

FABRIC	NO. OF PIECES	SIZE	CUTTING MARK	TOTAL NO. FULL BIAS STRIPS	STRIP UNIT
Purple	1	11" x 41"	4¾"	6	I
	1	11" x 16½"			
Orange	1	10" x 21¼"	3"	3	II
Black floral	1	11" x 35¼"	2¾"	7	I
Peach	1	10" x 21¼"	3"	3	II

Using the Bias Stripper, cut the number of full bias strips indicated in the chart. If you are right-handed, cut all fabrics face up. If you are left-handed, cut all fabrics face down. Reserve 1 black floral, 1 peach, and 1 orange corner triangle to use during quilt construction.

 Purple   Orange   Black floral   Peach   Teal #1   Teal #2   Black   Border print

Piecing the Blocks

Press seam allowances in the direction of the arrows unless otherwise instructed.

1. Assemble 1 Strip Unit I. Draw a chalk line through the center of each purple bias strip. Align the 2" mark on the short side of the Bias Stripper with the seam line. See page 18 for directions on marking the center of these strips. Cut 12 center-stripe squares, each 4⅞" x 4⅞".

Strip Unit I
Make 1.   Cut 12.

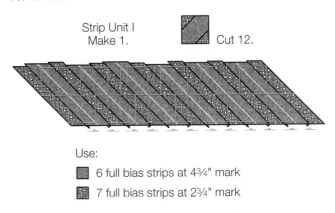

Use:
- 6 full bias strips at 4¾" mark
- 7 full bias strips at 2¾" mark

2. Using the Bias Stripper, cut 1 reserved peach and 1 reserved orange corner triangle into corner bias strips at the 3" mark. Using the corner bias strips and the full bias strips cut previously, assemble 1 Strip Unit II. Cut 24 bias squares, each 2⅞" x 2⅞".

Strip Unit II
Make 1.   Cut 24.

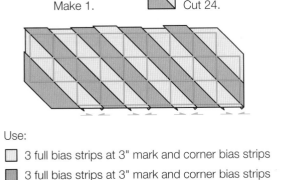

Use:
- 3 full bias strips at 3" mark and corner bias strips
- 3 full bias strips at 3" mark and corner bias strips

3. Cut the 11" black floral square once diagonally to make 2 triangles. Add the reserved black floral triangle to the stack. Cut the two 11" teal squares once diagonally to make 4 triangles (you will use only 3). Pair each of the 3 teal triangles with a black floral triangle, placing right sides together. Align the long bias edges and 1 set of points. Using the Bias Stripper, cut 2 bias strips from each triangle pair at the 3" mark. Join the

paired strips along their long bias edges and assemble 1 Strip Unit III. Cut 20 bias squares, each 2⅞" x 2⅞".

Strip Unit III
Make 1.   Cut 20.

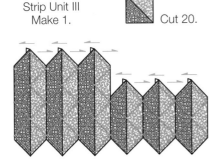

4. Cut each bias square once diagonally to make side-by-sides. Cut the center-stripe squares in half on the chalk line to make center-stripe triangles.

5. Arrange and then sew the black floral/teal side-by-side triangles into 20 triangle patches.

Make 20.

6. Sew a 2½" peach square to each of the triangle patches as shown.

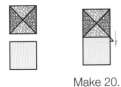

Make 20.

7. Sew a pair of orange/peach side-by-sides to a 2½" peach square. Sew this unit to a center-stripe triangle.

Make 24.

8. Assemble 5 Desert Dog blocks as shown.

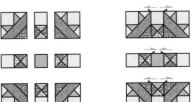

Make 5.

 Purple   Orange   Black floral   Peach   Teal #1   Teal #2   Black   Border print

Assembling and Finishing the Quilt Top

1. Cut each 7¼" peach square twice diagonally to make 20 side-setting triangles. Assemble 4 pieced side-setting triangles as shown. Trim the diagonal edge to ¼" from the black squares.

Trim to ¼" from corners of squares.

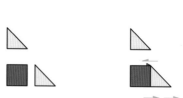

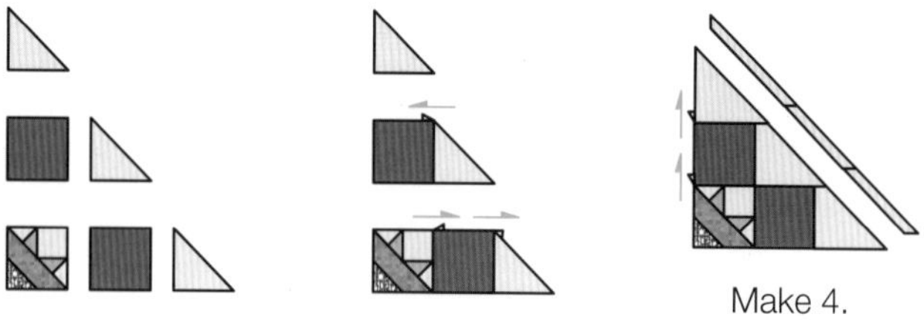

Make 4.

2. Cut each 5½" peach square once diagonally to make 4 corner-setting triangles. Using these half-square triangles, the remaining 8 peach side-setting triangles, and the black 4½" x 6½" rectangles, assemble 4 corner-setting triangles as shown.

Make 4 pieced corners.

3. Make 2 end rows as shown. Press the seam allowances toward the sashing strips.

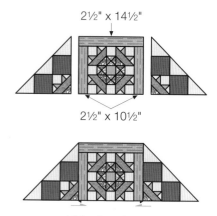

2½" x 14½"

2½" x 10½"

Make 2 end rows.

4. Make 1 center row as shown. Press the seam allowances toward the sashing strips.

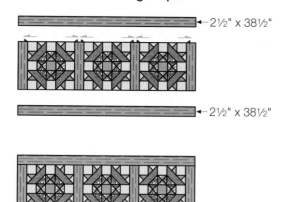

2½" x 38½"

2½" x 38½"

Make 1 center row.

5. Sew the rows together, adding the corner-setting triangles last.

End row

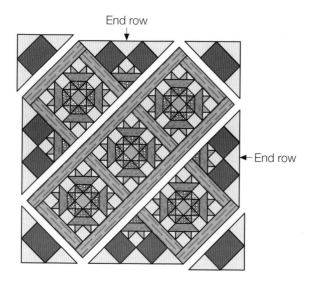

End row

6. Attach the inner and outer borders. If you have a strong directional print like the one in "Desert Dogs," shown on page 30, you should miter the borders. See "Mitered Borders" on page 91. If you do not need to miter your borders, measure the quilt top, cut the border strips to size, and then sew the strips to the quilt top, referring to "Plain Borders" on page 91.

7. Referring to "Quilt Finishing" on pages 91–96, layer the completed quilt top with batting and backing; baste. Quilt as desired. Bind the edges of the quilt. Add a label.

 Purple   Orange   Black floral   Peach   Teal #1   Teal #2   Black   Border print

Amish Puzzle

Color Photo on Page 27 ◆ Finished Quilt Size: 62¾" x 62¾" ◆ Finished Block Size: 8" x 8"

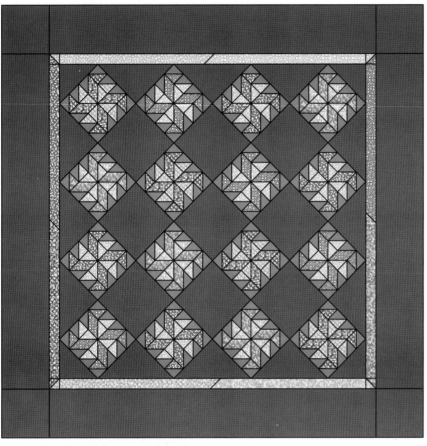

This quilt has sixteen blocks, four each of four dark-medium color combinations. Each group of four blocks has a different dark blue background, and all the blocks are set together with plain black alternating squares and side-setting triangles. You can easily change the size of this quilt by adding or subtracting quartets of blocks. Bias squares give the same effect of a mitered border with less fuss. The pieced binding of the quilt shown on page 27 mimics the style of the border. If you prefer not to piece the binding, you need ½ yard of fabric.

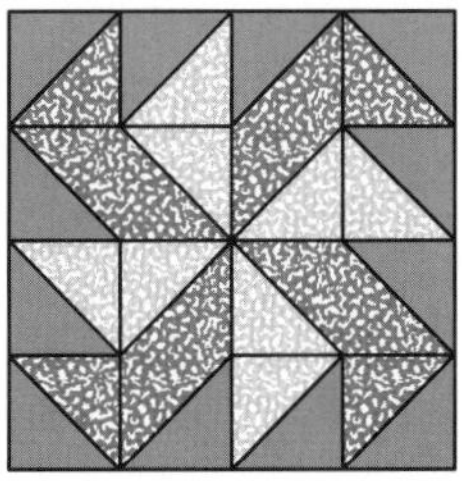

Materials: 44"-wide fabric

½ yd. *each of 4 darks and 4 mediums for 4 different color combinations (gold, purple, red, and teal)*

½ yd. *each of 4 dark blues*

2⅝ yds. black

4 yds. for backing

Amish Puzzle

▦	Dark gold
▢	Medium gold
▦	Dark purple
▦	Medium purple
▦	Dark red
▢	Medium red
▦	Dark teal
▢	Medium teal
▮	Dark blues
▮	Black

Cutting

From *each* dark and medium fabric, cut:
  1 piece, 11" x 22", for Strip Unit I
  1 strip, 2" x 26", for pieced border
  5 strips, each 2" x 9", for pieced binding

From *each* dark blue fabric, cut:
  1 strip, 11" x 18", for Strip Unit I
  1 square, 11" x 11", for Strip Unit II

From the black fabric, cut:
  3 strips, each 8½" x 41"; crosscut into
    9 squares, each 8½" x 8½", for plain blocks
    4 squares, each 7½" x 7½", for border corner
      squares
  1 strip, 7" x 41"; crosscut into 2 squares, each
    7" x 7", for corner-setting triangles
  1 strip, 13" x 41"; crosscut into 3 squares, each
    13" x 13", for side-setting triangles
  5 strips, each 7½" x 41", for outer border

Bias Strip Cutting Chart for Each Four-Block Combination

FABRIC	NO. OF PIECES	SIZE	CUTTING MARK	TOTAL NO. FULL BIAS STRIPS	STRIP UNIT
Dark	1	11" x 22"	2"	4	I
Medium	1	11" x 22"	2¾"	3	I
Dark blue	1	11" x 18"	2¾"	2	I

Using the Bias Stripper, cut the number of full bias strips indicated in the chart. If you are right-handed, cut all fabrics face up. If you are left-handed, cut all fabrics face down. Reserve 2 dark, 2 medium, and 2 dark blue corner triangles to use during quilt construction.

Piecing a Pair of Blocks

Press seam allowances in the direction of the arrows unless otherwise instructed.

1. Assemble 1 Strip Unit I. Cut 16 striped rectangles, each 2½" x 4½".

2. Cut the 11" dark blue square once diagonally to make 2 triangles. Add the triangles to the 2 reserved dark blue corner triangles. Pair each dark blue triangle with a reserved dark or medium corner triangle, placing right sides together. Align the bias edges and 1 set of points. Using the Bias Stripper, cut each triangle pair twice at the 2¾" mark. Join the paired strips along their long bias edges and assemble them into 4 Strip Unit II; 2 for each dark and medium color. Cut 16 bias squares, each 2½" x 2½", from each color combination.

Strip Unit I
Make 1.

 Cut 16.

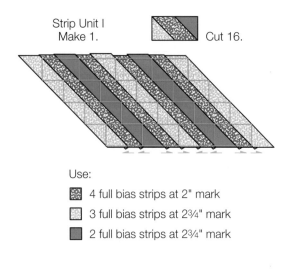

Use:
  ▨ 4 full bias strips at 2" mark
  ▢ 3 full bias strips at 2¾" mark
  ■ 2 full bias strips at 2¾" mark

Strip Unit II
Make 1 each coloration.

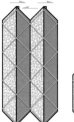 Cut 16.   Cut 16.

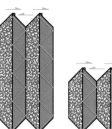

3. Sew a dark and a medium bias square together as shown. Sew this unit to a striped rectangle.

Make 16. Make 16.

4. Assemble 4 Amish Puzzle blocks as shown.

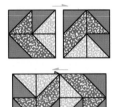 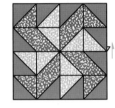

Make 4.

5. Repeat steps 1–4 for each dark-medium color combination to make a total of 16 blocks.

Assembling and Finishing the Quilt Top

1. Cut the 13" black squares twice diagonally to make 12 side-setting triangles. Arrange the Amish Puzzle blocks, the 8½" black squares, and the side-setting triangles into rows as shown. Sew the units together and press the seam allowances toward the plain squares and side-setting triangles. Join the rows. Press.

2. Cut each 7" black square once diagonally to make 4 corner-setting triangles. Sew them to the corners of the quilt top. Press the seam allowances toward the triangles. Trim the quilt top to ¼" from the block corners.

3. Arrange the various 2" x 26" border pieces around the edge of the quilt top until you find an arrangement that pleases you (see the quilt shown on page 27). Use 2 strips for each border. Place the strips together at right angles, and then draw a pencil line across the outside diagonal. Stitch on the line. Trim ¼" from the seam. Press. Sew the remaining border strips for each side in the same manner.

    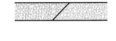

4. Measure the width of the quilt top through the center. Cut each pieced border to this dimension, keeping the seam centered on the border. (*Hint:* Fold the border in half at the seam and cut it to half the center width from the fold.) Put the borders back in place around the quilt top and cut a 3" square of each color you are using. Cut the squares once diagonally to make triangles; you need 1 dark and 1 medium triangle of each color. Pair the triangles that will meet at each of the border's 4 corners. Sew the triangles together along their bias edges and press in either direction. Cut each triangle pair into a 2" bias square.

Cut 2" bias square.

5. Sew 2 border strips to opposite sides of the quilt top. Press the seam allowances toward the border. Sew the corresponding corner bias squares to the ends of the 2 remaining borders. Press the seam allowances toward the border. Sew the borders to the top and bottom edges of the quilt top. Press the seam allowances toward the borders.

 Dark gold   Medium gold   Dark purple   Medium purple   Dark red   Medium red   Dark teal   Medium teal   Dark blues Black

6. Measure the width of the quilt top through the center. Join the 5 black 7½" x 41" strips into 1 long strip, and cut 4 border strips to match the quilt width. Sew 2 border strips to opposite sides of the quilt top. Press the seam allowances toward the black border. Sew a 7½" square to each end of the remaining 2 borders, and press the seam allowances toward the border strips. Sew the 2 remaining borders to the top and bottom edges. Press the seam allowances toward the black border.

7. Referring to "Quilt Finishing" on pages 91–96, layer the completed quilt top with batting and backing; baste. Quilt as desired. Trim excess batting and backing when done.

8. Make a pieced binding from the 2" x 9" strips. Lay the strips around the perimeter of the quilt in a pleasing arrangement. Sew them together with diagonal seams as you did for the pieced border in step 3 of "Assembling and Finishing the Quilt." Press the binding in half along its length, and then pin it to the quilt top to make sure no seams will fall at a corner of the quilt, which would make it hard to turn the binding. Take in a little on several seams, if necessary, to make sure the binding's starting and stopping strips will be similar in size to the others when sewn in place. Refer to "Binding the Quilt" on page 95. Add a label.

Starweave

Color Photo on Page 31 ◈ Finished Size: 60¹/₂" x 60¹/₂" ◈ Finished Block Size: 8" x 8"

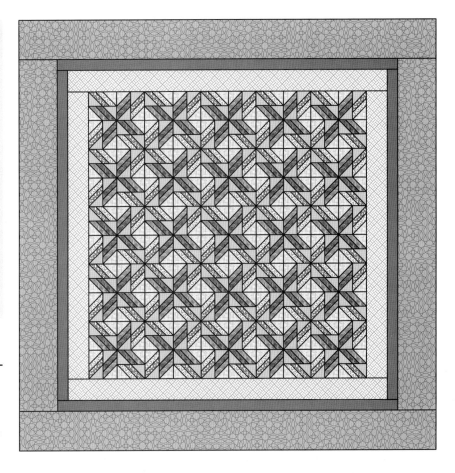

*Y*ou can soften the graphic lines of this quilt with warm tones and plaids, or you can highlight them with bright colors on a black background. No matter what your choice of fabrics, the blocks are easily assembled from pairs of striped rectangles. One note, though: if your seams are not accurate, you may have trouble matching intersections. Make sure to check your seam guide twice before starting this quilt! Beyond that, it's an easy quilt to cut and assemble.

Materials: 44"-wide fabric

1 piece *each* of 6 dark blue prints and 6 medium blue prints, each 10" x 21"

1 piece *each* of 6 dark red prints and 6 medium red prints, each 10" x 21"

³/₈ yd. *each* of 5 gold prints

³/₈ yd. *each* of 5 tan prints

⁵/₈ yd. tan print

³/₈ yd. navy blue print

1¹/₈ yds. dark paisley print

¹/₂ yd. for binding

3⁷/₈ yds. for backing

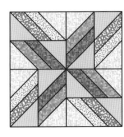

Starweave

■ Dark blues

■ Medium blues

■ Dark reds

□ Medium reds

□ Golds

□ Assorted tans

⊠ Tan print

■ Navy blue

▦ Dark paisley

Cutting

All measurements include ¼"-wide seam allowances.

From *each* dark blue and medium blue print, cut:
1 piece, 9" x 20", for Strip Unit I

From *each* dark red and medium red print, cut:
1 piece, 9" x 20", for Strip Unit II

From *each* of the 5 gold prints, cut:
1 piece, 9" x 37", for Strip Units I and II

From *each* of the 5 tan prints, cut:
1 piece, 9" x 37", for Strip Units I and II

From the ⅝-yard length of tan print, cut:
5 strips, each 3½" x 41", for inner border

From the navy blue print, cut:
5 strips, each 2" x 41", for middle border

From the dark paisley print, cut:
6 strips, each 6" x 41", for outer border

From the fabric for binding, cut:
7 strips, each 2" x 41"

Bias Strip Cutting Chart

FABRIC	NO. OF PIECES	SIZE	CUTTING MARK	TOTAL NO. FULL BIAS STRIPS	STRIP UNIT
Dark blues	6	9" x 20"	1"	36	I
Medium blues	6	9" x 20"	1"	36	I
Dark reds	6	9" x 20"	1"	36	II
Medium reds	6	9" x 20"	1"	36	II
Golds	5	9" x 37"	2¾"	40	I, II
Tans	5	9" x 37"	2¾"	40	I, II

Using the Bias Stripper, cut the number of full bias strips indicated in the chart. If you are right-handed, cut all fabrics face up. If you are left-handed, cut all fabrics face down. Set aside the corner triangles for a pieced backing or for another project.

Piecing the Blocks

Press seam allowances in the direction of the arrows unless otherwise indicated.

1. Assemble 4 Strip Unit I. Cut a total of 100 striped rectangles, each 2½" x 4½".

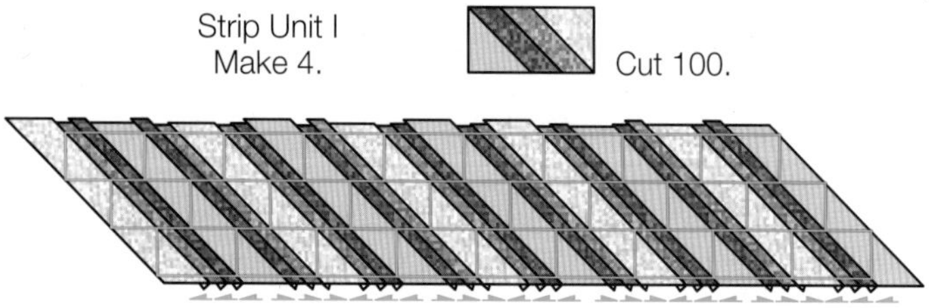

Strip Unit I
Make 4.

 Cut 100.

For each strip unit, use:

▨ 5 full bias strips at 2¾" mark
▨ 9 full bias strips at 1" mark
▨ 9 full bias strips at 1" mark
▢ 5 full bias strips at 2¾" mark

2. Assemble 4 Strip Unit II. Cut a total of 100 striped rectangles, each 2½" x 4½".

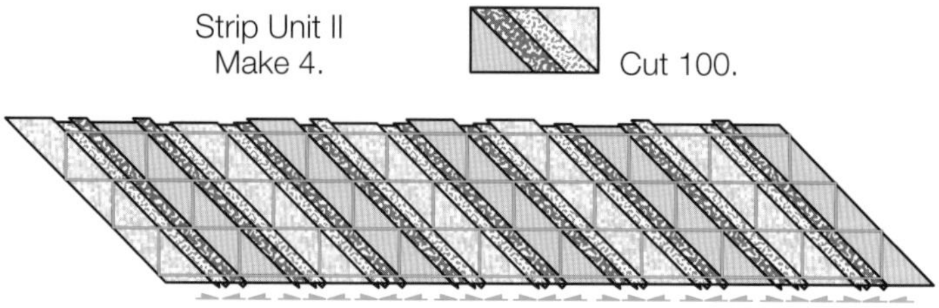

Strip Unit II
Make 4.

 Cut 100.

For each strip unit, use:

▢ 5 full bias strips at 2¾" mark
▨ 9 full bias strips at 1" mark
▨ 9 full bias strips at 1" mark
▢ 5 full bias strips at 2¾" mark

 Dark blues   Medium blues   Dark reds   Medium reds   Golds   Assorted tans   Tan print   Navy blue   Dark paisley

3. Sew each blue-striped rectangle to a red-striped rectangle as shown.

Make 100.

4. Assemble 25 Starweave blocks as shown. Butt diagonal seams when stitching. Press the final seam in either direction.

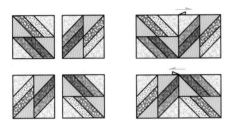

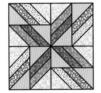

Make 25.

Assembling and Finishing the Quilt Top

1. Arrange the blocks in 5 rows of 5 blocks each, alternating the direction of the middle seam from block to block. Sew the blocks together, pressing the seams in opposite directions from row to row. Join the rows. Press.

2. Referring to "Plain Borders" on page 91, measure the quilt top, cut the tan border strips to size, then sew the strips to the quilt top. Repeat for the navy blue middle border and the dark paisley outer border.

3. Referring to "Quilt Finishing" on pages 91–96, layer the quilt top with batting and backing; baste. Quilt as desired. Bind the edges of the quilt. Add a label.

 Dark blues   Medium blues   Dark reds   Medium reds   Golds   Assorted tans   Tan print   Navy blue   Dark paisley

TILE PUZZLE

Color Photo on Page 30 ◈ Finished Quilt Size: 67" x 91" ◈ Finished Block Size: 6" x 6"

*S*ince this is a scrappy quilt, it would be great if you could cut each piece from a different print. Since most of us don't have such a fabric stash, I've provided a guideline that will give your quilt enough diversity to make it interesting.

To simplify fabric selection, choose two main color families. Select twelve medium-dark prints from each. Select nine very dark multicolored prints that include both color families. These very dark prints will be the nine-patch center squares that create the transparent effect where color families cross. Choose twelve light prints from both color families for the background.

The border is made up of on-point squares, and you'll need to use the Bias Stripper when cutting them. See "On-Point Squares and Bias Squares" on page 24.

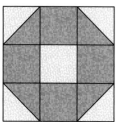

Block A

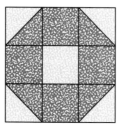

Block B

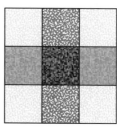

Block C

Medium-dark teals

Medium-dark purples

Lights

Very dark multicolored

Medium teal

Border print

Materials: 44"-wide fabrics

1 fat quarter *each* of 12 medium-dark teal prints

1 fat quarter *each* of 12 medium-dark purple prints

½ yd. *each* of 12 light prints

1 piece *each* of 9 very dark multicolored prints, each
9" x 20" (or ⅞ yd. of 1 print). Each print should include
both teal and purple elements.

⅝ yd. medium teal print for inner border

¾ yd. dark print for outer border

⅝ yd. for binding

5½ yds. for backing

Cutting

All measurements include ¼"-wide seam allowances.

From the 12 medium-dark teal prints, cut a total of:

12 pieces, each 6" x 13", for Strip Unit V (1 from
each print)

28 strips, each 2½" x 20", for Strip Units I and IV
(2 from each print plus 4 more from leftovers)

70 squares, each 2½" x 2½", for blocks (6 from
each print)

**From the 12 medium-dark purple prints, cut
a total of:**

8 pieces, each 6" x 13", for Strip Unit VI

25 strips, each 2½" x 20", for Strip Units II and III
(2 from each print plus 1 more from leftovers)

48 squares, each 2½" x 2½", for blocks (4 from
each print)

From the 12 light prints, cut a total of:

20 pieces, each 6" x 13", for Strip Units V and VI
(1 from each print plus 8 more from leftovers)

43 strips, each 2½" x 20", for Strip Units I, II, and III
(3 from each print plus 7 more from leftovers)

72 squares, each 3¼" x 3¼", for border triangles
(6 from each print)

**From the very dark multicolored prints, cut
a total of:**

9 strips, each 2½" x 20", for Strip Unit IV (1 from
each print)

144 squares, each cut at the 2" mark of the Bias
Stripper (16 from each print) *Hint:* Using the Bias
Stripper, cut 2 straight-grain strips from each print
at the 2" mark. Cut squares from each strip at the
2" mark.

From the medium teal print, cut:

7 strips, each 2½" x 41", for inner border

From the dark print, cut:

8 strips, each 2¾" x 41", for outer border

From the fabric for binding, cut:

8 strips, each 2" x 41"

Piecing the Blocks

Press seam allowances in the direction of the
arrows unless otherwise instructed.

1. Assemble Strip Units I–IV as shown. Cut the indicated number of 2½" segments from each strip unit.

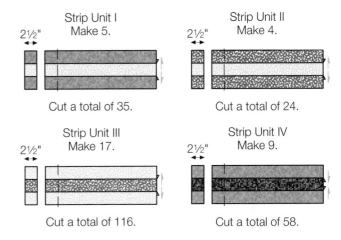

Strip Unit I
Make 5.
2½"
Cut a total of 35.

Strip Unit II
Make 4.
2½"
Cut a total of 24.

Strip Unit III
Make 17.
2½"
Cut a total of 116.

Strip Unit IV
Make 9.
2½"
Cut a total of 58.

2. Using the Bias Stripper, cut the 12 medium-dark
teal, 8 medium-dark purple, and 20 light 6" x 13"
pieces print-side up into 2 full bias strips, each at the
2¾" mark. To save time, stack several prints and cut
them all at once. Reserve all corner triangles.

3. Using the full bias strips and corner triangles from
step 2, assemble 24 Strip Unit V and 16 Strip Unit VI.
Mix and match the prints of the same color in each
strip unit to make them scrappier. Cut a total of 140
bias squares, each 2½" x 2½", from Strip Unit V. Cut a
total of 96 bias squares, each 2½" x 2½", from Strip
Unit VI.

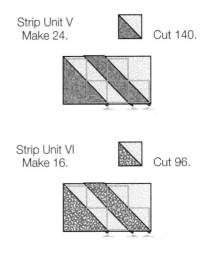

Strip Unit V
Make 24.
Cut 140.

Strip Unit VI
Make 16.
Cut 96.

 Medium-
dark teals

 Medium-
dark purples

 Lights

 Very dark
multicolored

 Medium teal

 Border print

4. Assemble 35 teal Block A and 24 purple Block B as shown.

Block A
Make 35.

Block B
Make 24.

5. Assemble 58 Block C as shown.

Block C
Make 58.

Assembling and Finishing the Quilt Top

1. Arrange Blocks A, B, and C in rows as shown; the line on the Block C squares indicates the horizontal or vertical direction of the purple center segment. Join the blocks into rows. Press the seam allowances toward Block C. Join the rows. Press.

A	C	A	C	A	C	A	C	A
C	B	C	B	C	B	C	B	C
A	C	A	C	A	C	A	C	A
C	B	C	B	C	B	C	B	C
A	C	A	C	A	C	A	C	A
C	B	C	B	C	B	C	B	C
A	C	A	C	A	C	A	C	A
C	B	C	B	C	B	C	B	C
A	C	A	C	A	C	A	C	A
C	B	C	B	C	B	C	B	C
A	C	A	C	A	C	A	C	A
C	B	C	B	C	B	C	B	C
A	C	A	C	A	C	A	C	A

2. Referring to "Plain Borders" on page 91, measure the quilt top, cut the medium-teal border strips to size, and then sew the strips to the quilt top.

3. Cut each 3¼" light square twice diagonally to make 288 quarter-square triangles. Sew 2 triangles to each of the very dark multicolored squares as shown to make 140 border units and 4 corner units.

Border units
Make 140.

Corner units
Make 4.

4. To make a side border, sew 41 border units together; add a corner unit to the right-hand end. Make 2 side borders. To make top and bottom borders, sew 29 border units together; add a corner unit to the right side. Make 2 borders. Press all seams to the right. Pin and sew the 4 borders to the sides of the quilt, starting and stopping exactly ¼" from each end. Press the seam allowances toward the inner border.

41 border units   Corner unit

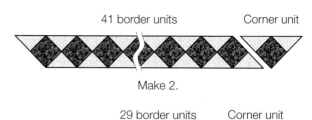

Make 2.

29 border units   Corner unit

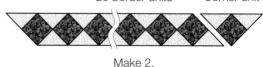

Make 2.

5. At each corner, place the border ends right sides together, aligning the diagonal edges and seams; pin. Stitch with a ¼"-wide seam allowance from the inside corner to the outer edge.

6. Measure the quilt top, cut the dark print strips to size, and then sew the strips to the quilt top as you did for the inner border.

7. Referring to "Quilt Finishing" on pages 91–96, layer the completed quilt top with batting and backing; baste. Quilt as desired. Bind the edges of the quilt. Add a label.

 Medium-dark teals   Medium-dark purples   Lights   Very dark multicolored   Medium teal   Border print

TOAD IN A PUDDLE

*M*ake this pretty quilt one block at a time. To add pizzazz, use a different purple print for each block.

For this pattern, you will use the Bias Stripper in conjunction with your standard rotary ruler to produce bias squares that measure 2" across the diagonal when finished. Refer to "On-Point Squares and Bias Squares" on page 24. Use a standard rotary-cutting ruler for all cutting except where instructed to use the Bias Stripper.

Have fun making this quilt as large or as small as you wish, one block at a time.

Materials: 44"-wide fabric

1 piece, 7" x 16", each of 9 purple prints

1 yd. light print

⅝ yd. dark green print

¼ yd. fuchsia print

⅝ yd. lavender floral

⅜ yd. for binding

1 yd. backing

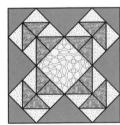

Toad in a Puddle

- Assorted purples
- Light
- Dark green
- Fuchsia
- Lavender floral

Cutting

All measurements include ¼"-wide seam allowances.

From *each* purple print, cut:
  1 piece, 5½" x 14", for bias strip piecing

From the light print, cut:
  9 pieces, each 5½" x 17", for bias strip piecing

From the dark green print, cut:
  9 squares, each 5¼" x 5¼", for blocks
  18 squares, each 2⅞" x 2⅞", for blocks

From the fuchsia print, cut:
  4 strips, each 1" x 26", for inner border

From the lavender floral, cut:
  1 strip selvage to selvage at the 4" mark on the Bias
    Stripper; crosscut into 9 squares, each cut at the
    4" mark on the Bias Stripper
  4 strips, each 3½" x 41", for outer border

From the fabric for binding, cut:
  4 strips, each 2" x 41"

Piecing One Block

Press seam allowances in the direction of the arrows unless otherwise instructed.

1. Using a standard rotary-cutting ruler, cut 4 full bias strips, each 2" wide, from 1 light 5½" x 17" piece, and 3 full bias strips, each 2" wide, from 1 purple 5½" x 14" piece. Reserve the 2 purple corner triangles.

2. Assemble a bias strip unit, adding the 2 reserved purple corner triangles at each end. Using the Bias Stripper, cut 16 bias squares at the 2" mark. See "On-Point Squares and Bias Squares" on page 24.

Bias Strip Unit I
Make 1.

 Cut 16 using Bias Stripper.

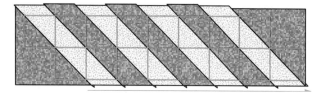

Use:

▨ 3 full bias strips cut 2" wide with regular ruler and 2 corner triangles

▢ 2 full bias strips cut 2" wide with regular ruler

3. Join the bias squares as shown. Pay close attention to the direction of the seam allowances.

Make 4.

4. Cut 1 dark green 5¼" square twice diagonally to make 4 side-setting triangles. Assemble 1 partial Toad in the Puddle block as shown.

Make 1.

5. Cut 2 dark green 2⅞" squares once diagonally to make 4 triangles. Sew a triangle to each corner of the block. Press 2 triangles on opposite corners away from the block and the other 2 toward the block. *Hint:* When placing the triangle on the corner, align the point of the triangle with the center seam of the bias square unit.

Make 1.

6. Repeat steps 1–5 to complete 9 blocks.

Assembling and Finishing the Quilt Top

1. Arrange the blocks in 3 rows of 3 blocks each. Turn the blocks once clockwise, if necessary, so that corner seams will butt when joined. Sew the blocks together. Press seams in alternate directions from row to row. Join the rows. Press.

2. Referring to "Plain Borders" on page 91, measure the quilt top, cut the fuchsia inner border strips to size, and then sew the strips to the quilt top. Repeat for the lavender outer border.

3. Referring to "Quilt Finishing" on pages 91–96, layer the quilt with batting and backing; baste. Quilt as desired. Bind the edges of the quilt. Add a label.

Assorted purples   Light   Dark green   Fuchsia   Lavender floral

Starlight Express

Color Photo on Page 34 ❖ Finished Quilt Size: 50" x 50" ❖ Finished Block Size: 9" x 9"

This beautiful quilt is an exercise in on-point construction techniques. Parts of the block are set on point and need to mesh with straight-set units. The pieced border is also set on point. Use a standard rotary ruler for all cutting, except when instructed to use the Bias Stripper. Please note in the Bias Strip Cutting Chart that you will sometimes use both types of rulers to cut bias strips from the same piece of fabric. Pay careful attention to avoid making mistakes. Refer to "On-Point Squares and Bias Squares" on page 24.

This quilt is the most challenging in the book, but only because it calls for so many techniques. The result is worth the effort!

Materials: 44"-wide fabric

¾ yd. dark red print

½ yd. medium red print

¾ yd. dark green print

½ yd. medium green print

¾ yd. floral

1 yd. light print

1⅜ yds. pink print

½ yd. for binding

3¼ yds. for backing

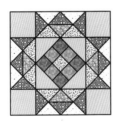

Variable Square

Sashing Square

Sashing A

Sashing B

▨ Dark red

▨ Medium red

▨ Dark green

▨ Medium green

▨ Floral

☐ Light

▨ Pink

Cutting

From the dark red print, cut:
   1 piece, 11" x 40", for Strip Units I and III
   5 strips, each cut selvage to selvage at the 1½" mark
      on the Bias Stripper, and crosscut into
      9 strips, each 20" long, for Strip Units VII, IX,
         and X
      2 strips, each 10" long, for Strip Units XI and XII

From the medium red print, cut:
   1 piece, 11" x 41"; crosscut into
      1 piece, 11" x 20", for Strip Unit III
      1 strip, 20" long, cut at the 1½" mark on the Bias
         Stripper, for Strip Unit VII
   2 strips, each 10" long, cut at the 1½" mark on the
      Bias Stripper, for Strip Unit VIII

From the dark green print, cut:
   1 piece, 11" x 25", for Strip Units II and IV
   6 strips, each cut selvage to selvage at the 1½" mark
      on the Bias Stripper; crosscut into 12 strips, each
      20" long, for Strip Units V, XIII, and XIV

From the medium green print, cut:
   1 piece, 11" x 14", for Strip Unit IV
   4 strips, each 20" long, cut at the 1½" mark on the
      Bias Stripper, for Strip Units V and VI

From the floral, cut:
   1 piece, 11" x 39", for Strip Units I and II
   7 strips, each cut selvage to selvage at the 1½" mark
      on the Bias Stripper; crosscut into
      12 strips, each 20" long, for Strip Units VI, IX, X,
         XIII, and XIV
      3 strips, each 10" long, for Strip Units VIII and XI

From the light print, cut:
   2 strips, each 5" x 41"; crosscut into
      8 rectangles, each 5" x 7¼", for pieced sashing
         strips
      4 squares, each 5" x 5", for pieced sashing strips
   3 strips, each 3½" x 41"; crosscut into a total of 26
      squares, each 3½" x 3½", for blocks and sashing
      strips
   4 strips, each 2¾" x 41", for inner border

From the pink print, cut:
   4 strips, each cut selvage to selvage at the 1½" mark
      on the Bias Stripper; crosscut into
      7 strips, each 20" long, for Strip Units IX and XIII
      2 strips, each 10" long, for Strip Unit XII
   3 strips, each 5¾" x 41"; crosscut into 18 squares,
      each 5¾" x 5¾", for pieced border
   3 strips, each 3⅛" x 41"; crosscut into 34 squares,
      each 3⅛" x 3⅛", for block centers, pieced
      sashing, and pieced border
   3 strips, each 2¾" x 41"; crosscut into 36 squares,
      each 2¾" x 2¾", for blocks

From the fabric for binding, cut:
   6 strips, each 2" x 41"

Bias Strip Cutting Chart

FABRIC	SIZE	TOOL	CUTTING MARK	STRIP WIDTH	TOTAL NO. FULL BIAS STRIPS	STRIP UNIT
Dark red	11" x 40"	Bias Stripper	3¼"		5	I
		Standard rotary ruler		2⅛"	3	III
Medium red	11" x 20"	Standard rotary ruler		2⅛"	3	III
Dark green	11" x 25"	Bias Stripper	3¼"		2	II
		Standard rotary ruler		2⅛"	2	IV
Medium green	11" x 14"	Standard rotary ruler		2⅛"	1	IV
Floral	11" x 39"	Bias Stripper	3¼"		7	I, II

Using both the Bias Stripper and a standard rotary ruler, cut the number of full bias strips indicated in the chart. If you are right-handed, cut all fabrics face up. If you are left handed, cut all fabrics face down. Reserve 2 dark red, 1 medium red, 1 dark green, 2 medium green, and 2 floral 11" corner triangles to use during quilt construction.

 Dark red   Medium red   Dark green   Medium green   Floral   Light   Pink

Piecing the Blocks

Press seam allowances in the direction of the arrows unless otherwise instructed.

1. Using the Bias Stripper, cut 1 reserved dark red and 1 reserved floral corner triangle into corner bias strips at the 3¼" mark. Use the corner bias strips and the full bias strips cut previously to assemble 1 Strip Unit I. Using the Bias Square ruler, cut 36 bias squares, each 3⅛" x 3⅛".

Strip Unit I
Make 1.

Cut 36.

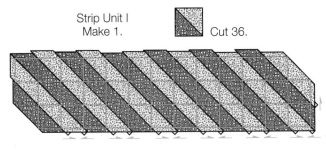

Use:

 5 full bias strips at 3¼" mark
 and corner bias strips at 3¼" mark

 5 full bias strips at 3¼" mark
 and corner bias strips at 3¼" mark

2. Using the Bias Stripper, cut 1 reserved dark green and 1 reserved floral corner triangle into corner bias strips at the 3¼" mark. Use the corner bias strips and the full bias strips cut previously to assemble 1 Strip Unit II. Using the Bias Square ruler, cut 16 bias squares, each 3⅛" x 3⅛".

Strip Unit II
Make 1.

Cut 16.

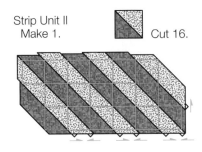

Use:

 2 full bias strips at 3¼" mark
 and corner bias strips at 3¼" mark

 2 full bias strips at 3¼" mark
 and corner bias strips at 3¼" mark

3. Using a standard rotary ruler, cut 1 reserved dark red and 1 reserved medium red corner triangle into 2⅛"-wide bias strips. Use the corner bias strips and the full bias strips cut previously to assemble 1 Strip Unit III. Using the Bias Stripper, cut 36 bias squares at the 2¼" mark.

Strip Unit III
Make 1.

Cut 36 using
the Bias Stripper.

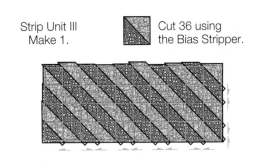

Use:

 3 full bias strips cut 2⅛" wide using a regular rotary ruler
 and corner bias strips cut 2⅛" wide.

 3 full bias strips cut 2⅛" wide using a regular rotary ruler
 and corner bias strips cut 2⅛" wide.

4. Using a standard rotary ruler, cut 1 long 2⅛"-wide corner bias strip from each of the 2 reserved medium green corner triangles. Use the corner bias strips and the full bias strips cut previously to assemble 1 Strip Unit IV. Using the Bias Stripper, cut 16 bias squares at the 2¼" mark.

Strip Unit IV
Make 1.

Cut 16 using
the Bias Stripper.

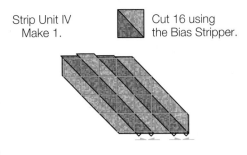

Use:

 2 full bias strips cut 2⅛" wide using a regular rotary ruler.

 1 full bias strip cut 2⅛" wide using a regular rotary ruler
 and 2 corner bias strips cut 2⅛" wide.

 Dark red   Medium red   Dark green   Medium green   Floral   Light   Pink

5. Cut each 3½" light square twice diagonally to make 104 quarter-square triangles. Sew 2 triangles to each dark red–medium red and dark green–medium green bias square. Make 36 red units and 16 green units.

Red Units
Make 36.

Green Units
Make 16.

6. Cut each red floral and green floral 3⅛" bias square once diagonally to make side-by-side triangles. Sew the red side-by-side units to the red units from step 5. Sew the green side-by-side units to the green units from step 5. Make 36 red pieced rectangles and 16 green pieced rectangles.

Make 36.

Make 16.

7. Assemble 2 Strip Unit V and 1 each of Strip Units VI, VII, and VIII. Cut the indicated number of segments from each strip unit at the 1½" mark on the Bias Stripper.

1½" mark

Strip Unit V
Make 2 strip units, each 20" long.

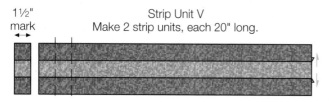

Cut 18 segments.

1½" mark

Strip Unit VI
Make 1 strip unit 20" long.

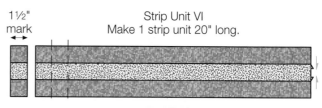

Cut 9 segments.

1½" mark

Strip Unit VII
Make 1 strip unit 20" long.

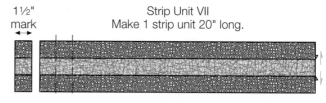

Cut 8 segments.

1½" mark

Strip Unit VIII
Make 1 strip unit 10" long.

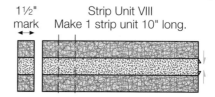

Cut 4 segments.

8. Cut 26 of the 3⅛" pink squares once diagonally to make 52 half-square triangles. Assemble 9 block centers and 4 sashing squares as shown. Press seam allowances toward the nine-patch units.

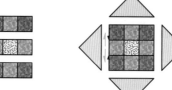 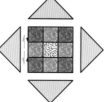

Make 9
block centers.

 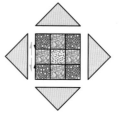

Make 4
sashing squares.

 Dark red   Medium red   Dark green   Medium green   Floral   Light   Pink

9. Assemble 9 Variable Square blocks as shown. Butt diagonal seams as well as straight seams when stitching.

Make 9.

Assembling and Finishing the Quilt Top

1. Make 8 Sashing A and 4 Sashing B as shown.

  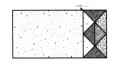

Make 8
Sashing A.

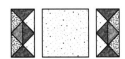 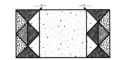

Make 4
Sashing B.

2. Arrange the Variable Square blocks, sashing squares, Sashing A, and Sashing B into rows as shown. Sew the units into rows. Press all seam allowances toward the sashing units. Join the rows. Press.

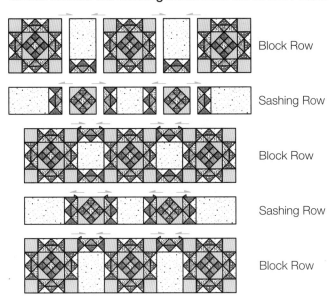

Block Row

Sashing Row

Block Row

Sashing Row

Block Row

3. Referring to "Plain Borders" on page 91, measure the quilt top, cut the light print border strips to size, and then sew the strips to the quilt top.

4. Assemble Strip Units IX–XIV as shown. Using the Bias Stripper, cut the indicated number of segments at the 1½" mark.

1½" mark

Strip Unit IX
Make 3 strip units, each 20" long.

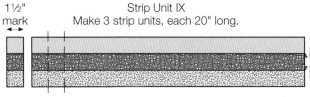

Cut 32 segments.

1½" mark

Strip Unit X
Make 2 strip units, each 20" long.

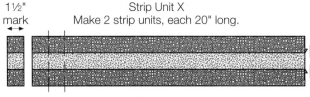

Cut 20 segments.

Strip Unit XI
1½" mark   Make 1 strip unit
10" long.

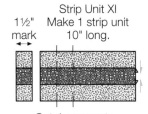

Cut 4 segments.

Strip Unit XII
1½" mark   Make 1 strip unit
10" long.

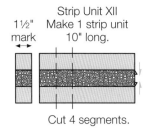

Cut 4 segments.

1½" mark

Strip Unit XIII
Make 4 strip units, each 20" long.

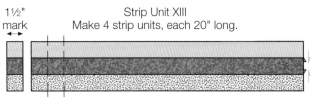

Cut 40 segments.

1½" mark

Strip Unit XIV
Make 2 strip units, each 20" long.

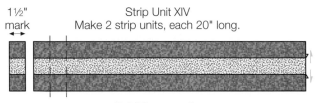

Cut 20 segments.

 Dark red   Medium red   Dark green   Medium green   Floral   Light   Pink

5. Assemble the 3 types of border nine-patch units as shown.

Make 20
green nine-patch units.

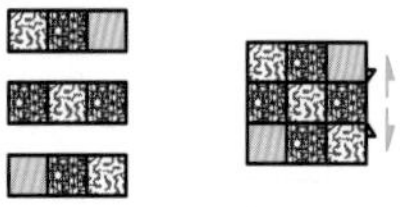

Make 16
red nine-patch units.

Make 4
border corner squares.

6. Cut the 18 pink 5¾" squares twice diagonally to make 72 quarter-square triangles. Make 16 red and 16 green slant units as shown.

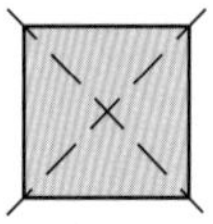

Make 16 green slants.   Make 16 red slants.

7. Cut the 8 remaining 3⅛" pink squares once diagonally to make 16 half-square triangles. Assemble 4 red and 4 green corners as shown.

Make 4
green corners.

Make 4
red corners.

8. Assemble the borders as shown. Sew the side borders to opposite sides of the quilt top. Press the seam allowances toward the inner border. Sew the top and bottom borders to the quilt top. Press the seam allowances toward the inner border.

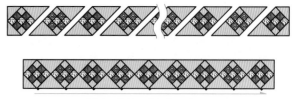

Make 2 for side borders.

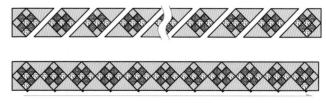

Make 2 for top and bottom borders.

9. Referring to "Quilt Finishing" on pages 91–96, layer the completed quilt top with batting and backing; baste. Quilt as desired. Bind the edges of the quilt. Add a label.

Dark red   Medium red   Dark green   Medium green   Floral   Light   Pink

QUILT FINISHING

Once your quilt top is done, you'll be anxious to finish your quilt. The following information is a brief overview of the basics. The Joy of Quilting series of books from That Patchwork Place addresses in depth each aspect of quiltmaking. I strongly encourage you to review these books for more extensive ideas on machine and hand quilting, setting quilts together, and binding edges.

Adding Borders

Straighten the edges of the quilt top before adding the borders. There should be little or no trimming needed for a straight-set quilt. A diagonally set quilt is often constructed with oversized side triangles, and you may need to trim these down to size. Align the ¼" line on the ruler with the block points and trim the quilt edges to ¼" from these points. Always position a ¼" line on the ruler along the block points of the adjacent edge at the same time, so that the corner will be square when the trimming is complete.

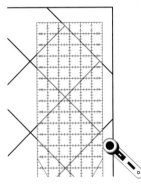

Trim the edges of the quilt to ¼" from the block points.

Plain Borders

To find the correct measurement for plain border strips, always measure through the center of the quilt, not at the outside edges. This ensures that the borders are of equal length on opposite sides of the quilt and brings the outer edges into line with the center dimension if discrepancies exist. Otherwise, your quilt might not be "square," due to minor piecing errors and/or stretching that can occur while you work with the pieces.

1. Sew the border strips together end to end to make one continuous strip. Measure the quilt from the top to the bottom edge through the center of the quilt. Cut two border strips from the long pieced strip to this measurement, and pin them to the sides of the quilt, easing to fit as necessary.

Center length

NOTE: If there is a large difference in the two sides or between the center and the sides, it is better to go back and correct the source of the problem now rather than try to make the border fit and end up with a distorted quilt later.

2. Sew the side borders in place and press the seams toward the borders.

3. Measure the center width of the quilt, including the side borders, to determine the length of the top and bottom border strips.

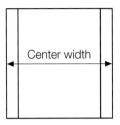

Center width

Cut the borders to this measurement, and pin them to the top and bottom of the quilt top, again easing to fit as needed. Stitch in place and press the seams toward the border strips.

Pieced Borders

It is easiest to apply pieced borders to quilt tops that are the proper size. If the quilt top is considerably different in size than it should be, it may be best to recalculate the number of pieced units to be used in the border or eliminate the pieced border altogether. Small differences in size can usually be accommodated.

1. Measure the center length of the quilt top. Measure the length of the pieced borders that will go on the sides of the quilt top. If they match, pin and sew the pieced borders to the sides of the quilt top, positioning any seams that need to be aligned with quilt-top seams. If there is a slight difference in the sizes of the borders and quilt sides, take in or let out a little from several seams on the pieced borders until they fit the dimensions of the quilt sides. Do not take in or let out only one seam or its difference in size will be very noticeable. A tiny adjustment in many seams will go unnoticed.

2. Follow the same procedure to measure the width of the quilt and to adjust and sew the top and bottom borders in place.

Mitered Borders

Mitered borders have diagonal seams sewn from the inner corner to the outer edge of the border strips.

1. Measure the width and length of the quilt top through the center. Double the width of your border strips and add this number to the quilt top measurements. Cut each border strip several inches longer than the combined measurements.

2. On the wrong side of the quilt top, mark ¼" in from each corner. Mark the center of each side.

3. Fold each border strip in half to find and mark the center. From the center mark, measure half the finished quilt-top measurement for the appropriate side and mark. For instance, if the quilt side measures 42" finished, measure 21" from either side of the border's center, and mark. The marks will center the border on the side of the quilt. You will have excess strip length on either side equal to the border width plus a couple of inches.

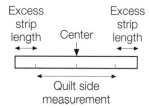

4. Pin the border strip to the side of the quilt, matching center and corner marks. Sew the border to the side of the quilt, using a ¼"-wide seam allowance; start, backstitch, and stop exactly at the ¼" marks at the corners. Measure, cut, and attach the 3 remaining borders in the same manner. Do not press the border yet.

5. To sew the mitered seam, fold the quilt top diagonally, wrong sides together, so the border strips lay on top of each other, right sides together. Align the excess strips.

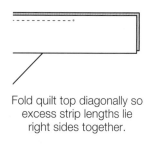

Fold quilt top diagonally so
excess strip lengths lie
right sides together.

6. Using the 45° angle on a ruler, draw a diagonal line from the border seams to the opposite raw edges of the strips. Pin, stitch, and backstitch on the diagonal line, beginning at the border seam and sewing out to the raw edges. Match any seams or fabric designs that converge at the seam.

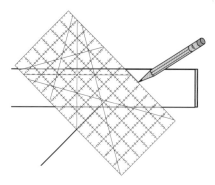

7. Check the accuracy and flatness of the mitered seam and make any adjustments before trimming ¼" from the seam.

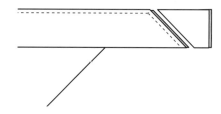

Choosing and Marking Quilting Designs

Quilting serves several purposes, the most important being to hold the three layers of the quilt together. Therefore, it is important to do an adequate amount of quilting, whether by hand or machine, to serve this purpose. The density of the quilting should be consistent so that one area of the quilt does not pucker or bulge as a result of too little or too much quilting. Keep this in mind when choosing your quilt designs—a heavily quilted border will also require heavy quilting in the interior.

There are a tremendous number of sources for quilting designs available commercially. Stencils are immensely popular and readily available. It's a simple matter to trace through the lines to mark the design you want. Other books deal exclusively with drawings of quilt designs that can be transferred in various ways to the quilt top. Simple overall designs such as cross-hatching, quilting in-the-ditch, outline quilting, and echo quilting are time-honored methods of quilting that do not require commercial stencils and books. Of course, you are free to design your own, too.

Many quilting designs must be marked directly on the quilt top to act as an accurate guide for your stitches. Choose nonpermanent markers for this task—I have seen the beauty of many a quilt ruined by permanent quilt markings. There is a wonderful assortment of wash-out markers available today. With all the time and expense put into the quilt top, it's a comparatively small expense to spend a few dollars on a good marker. Be sure to test a new marker on scrap fabric for washability before using it on your quilt top.

Before marking, press the quilt top one final time. Mark on a hard flat surface, keeping your marker sharp and your lines clear and fine. It's best to mark the quilt top all at one time, but sometimes it is not possible, and you may need to mark your top as you quilt. If this is the case, do your best to keep the lines from smudging as you will be marking on a padded surface.

Making a Quilt Backing

The quilt backing is sometimes called the lining. It is the back of the quilt. It must be cut 3" to 4" wider than the quilt top on all sides to allow for any shifting during the quilting process. To determine the size of the quilt backing you need, whether plain or pieced, measure the finished quilt top and add 6" to both length and width. For example, a quilt top that measures 38" x 54" requires a 44" x 60" backing.

The simplest quilt backings to make are plain backings. Many hand quilters prefer this type because there aren't any seams to quilt through. A plain backing is one piece of fabric without any seams. Plain or printed muslins are available in a number of different widths to accommodate all but the largest-size quilts. Choose a width larger than the width of the quilt backing to allow for shrinkage. To figure how many yards you need, convert the quilt-backing length to yards (divide by 36). Round this figure up to the nearest 1/8 yard and add another 1/8 yard for shrinkage. Purchase this amount.

A paneled backing is similar to a plain backing except that it is pieced in two or three vertical panels. The patterns in this book contain yardage to make paneled backings, using standard 44"-wide fabric that shrinks to approximately 42". If your quilt measures more than 42" wide, then you need two panels. Three panels are needed for a quilt wider than 84". Figure

yardage by doubling or tripling the quilt-backing length, depending on the number of panels needed. Divide this figure by 36, round up to the nearest 1/8 yard, and add another 1/8 yard for shrinkage.

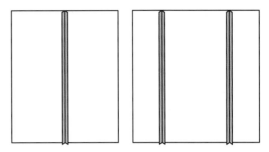

Two ways to piece paneled backings

An increasingly popular and fun way to make a quilt backing is to piece one. It can be pieced from large squares, triangles, rectangles, and "mistakes" left over from the quilt top or even other coordinating prints that you have on hand. No matter what you do, it is considerably less expensive, uses leftovers, and is totally delightful to discover on the back of a quilt.

Basting the Quilt Layers

The quilt sandwich is composed of the quilt top, backing, and a filler material called the batting. There are many battings available in both synthetic and natural fibers. Entire books are devoted to the advantages and disadvantages of the different types. Whatever batting you choose, be sure to read and follow the manufacturer's instructions on any preparation that may need to be done. The batting should be the same size as your backing. I open packaged batting and lay it flat and covered (I have cats!) on a bed overnight to relax the wrinkles and creases.

Once the quilting designs are marked, the backing is made, and a batting is bought and prepared, you are ready to secure the three layers with basting. Press the backing smooth and tape it, right side down, to a hard, clean, flat work surface such as a table or floor. Do not use a surface that you don't want marred with pin marks! Securely tape the sides of the backing every few inches. Tape the corners last, being careful not to stretch the bias. Smooth and center the batting over the backing. Carefully place the quilt top over the batting right side up. Smooth it and begin pin basting it to the other layers, always working from the center out. This will work out any unevenness in the layers.

For hand quilting, use a light-colored thread to baste the sandwich in a 3" to 4" grid, again working from the center out. Baste across both diagonals of the sandwich to stabilize the bias. Finish by securing the edges of the quilt sandwich with a line of stitches around the edge. Remove the pins.

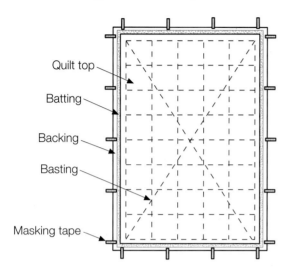

Many machine quilters and even some hand quilters prefer special quilter's safety pins to baste the sandwich instead of thread. Recently, some quilters have begun to use plastic tacks like those used to secure price tags to clothing. They are available at quilt and hobby shops or through mail-order catalogs.

Quilting

I have no expertise in machine quilting and recommend you refer to books by experts in that field for how-to information. *Machine Quilting Made Easy* by Maurine Noble (That Patchwork Place) is a good resource. I do hand quilt, though, and will briefly review the basics.

Quilting is a simple running stitch that goes through all three layers of the quilt sandwich. All quilting should be done from the center out. Most quilters prefer to use some type of frame to hold the three layers together when quilting to prevent shifting.

Quilting needles are called Betweens and come in different sizes. The larger the number, the smaller the needle and the smaller your stitches. Try to use the smallest needle you can comfortably handle. The

eyes are tiny, so many people use a needle threader to thread them. Use cotton hand-quilting thread cut into 12" to 18" lengths. Longer threads will weaken from sliding through the eye continuously. I strongly recommend that you use a thimble on your stitching finger. Some quilters also use one on the "receiving" finger under the quilt.

1. Begin quilting with a small single knot tied close to the end of the thread. Slip the needle between the layers of the quilt about a needle length's distance from your chosen starting point. If possible, weave the needle through a seam allowance. Bring the needle up where you want to start and give the thread a tug to lodge the knot in the batting or seam.

2. Following the quilting marks, sew a simple running stitch, being sure to catch all three layers with each stitch. Ideally, the stitches on the back of the quilt should be the same size as the stitches on the front. All stitches should be of consistent size and evenly spaced. This can take some practice. It is better to sacrifice small stitch size in favor of even spacing and consistent size.

3. End a line of quilting by forming a small knot in the thread about ⅛" from where it exits the quilt. Take the last stitch between the layers only and run the needle a short distance away from the last stitch before bringing the needle up, out of the quilt. Again, weaving the thread in and out of a seam allowance before exiting will strengthen the quilting. Give a gentle tug, and the knot will slip between the layers. Clip the thread a short distance from the quilt top and let the tail slip back between the layers.

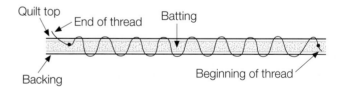

4. Work from the center of the quilt toward the edges to ease out any fullness. Finish all the quilting and remove the interior basting stitches before binding the quilt. Leave the perimeter basting stitches in place to hold the edges for the binding.

Binding the Quilt

The fabric requirements for the bindings in this book are based on straight-grain fabric strips for a double-fold binding, which is simple but durable.

NOTE: If you want to attach a sleeve or rod pocket to the back of the quilt, see page 96 for making the sleeve before you attach the binding.

1. Cut 2"-wide strips from selvage to selvage for a standard ¼"-wide finished binding.

2. Join the strips at right angles and stitch across the corner. Make one long piece of binding. Trim excess fabric and press seams open. It is important to use closely matching threads in this situation to avoid peekaboo stitches at the seams.

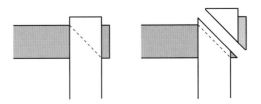

3. Fold the strip in half lengthwise, wrong sides together, and press. At one end of the strip, turn under ¼" at a 45° angle and press.

Fold line

To attach the binding:

1. Baste the three layers of the quilt securely at the outer edges if you have not already done so.

2. Trim the batting and backing even with the quilt top edges and corners.

3. In the center of one edge of the quilt, align the raw edges of the binding with the raw edge of the quilt top. Leaving about 6" free as a starting tail, sew the binding to the edge of the quilt with a ¼"-wide seam allowance. Stop stitching ¼" from the corner of the first side. (It's a good idea to pin-mark ¼" in from the corner before you begin sewing.) Backstitch and remove the quilt from the machine.

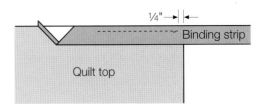
¼" Binding strip

Quilt top

4. To create a mitered turn at the corner, flip the binding straight up from the corner so that it forms a continuous line with the adjacent side of the quilt top.

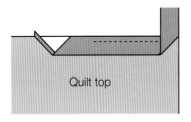
Quilt top

5. Fold the binding straight down so it lies on top of the adjacent side, being careful not to shift the pleat formed at the fold. Pin the pleat in place. Pin-mark ¼" in from the next corner. Starting at the edge, stitch the second side of the binding to the quilt, stopping at the ¼" mark. Flip up, then down, repeating the same process for the remaining corners.

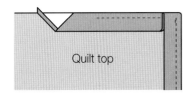
Quilt top

6. Repeat on the remaining edges and corners of the quilt. When you reach the beginning, overlap the binding by about 1". Cut away any excess binding, trimming the end at a 45° angle. Tuck the end into the fold and finish the seam.

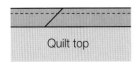
Quilt top

7. Turn the binding to the back of the quilt. Slipstitch the fold of the binding to the quilt backing. Slipstitch the miters in place on both front and back to complete the binding—and your quilt!

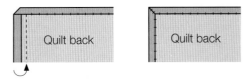
Quilt back   Quilt back

Adding a Sleeve

You will need to add a hanging sleeve if you plan to display your finished quilt on the wall.

1. Using leftover fabric or a piece of muslin, cut a strip 6" to 8" wide and 1" shorter than the width of the quilt at the top edge. Fold the ends under ¼", then under ¼" again, and stitch.

2. Fold the fabric strip in half lengthwise, wrong sides together, and baste the raw edges to the top edge of the back of your quilt. The top edge of the sleeve will be secured when the binding is sewn onto the quilt.

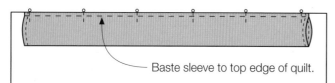

Baste sleeve to top edge of quilt.

3. Finish the sleeve after the binding has been attached by blindstitching the bottom of the sleeve in place. Push the bottom edge of the sleeve up just a bit to provide a little give so the hanging rod does not put strain on the quilt itself.

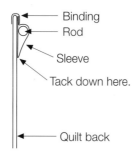

Binding
Rod
Sleeve
Tack down here.

Quilt back

Labeling Your Quilt

Be sure to sign and date your quilt. Labels can be elaborate or simple, and can be handwritten, typed, or embroidered. Be sure to include the name of the quilt, your name, your city and state, the date, and the name of the recipient if it is a gift. Add any other interesting or important information about the quilt. Future generations will be interested to know more about the quilt than just who made it and when.

ABOUT THE AUTHOR

Born and raised in southeastern Pennsylvania, Donna Lynn Thomas has had a needle in her hand since she was a little girl. Her mother was a home economics teacher and her father an engineer. It seems only natural that Donna, with a love for both fabric and geometry, would take to quilting.

Donna has been quilting since 1975 and teaching since 1982. The introduction of rotary-cutting tools in the 1980s revolutionized her approach to quiltmaking. Since Nancy J. Martin introduced her to bias strip piecing in 1987, Donna has worked exclusively with that method, developing new and innovative ways to maximize precision piecing. In 1995 Donna presented her tool, the Bias Stripper ruler, designed for use in conjunction with her bias strip-piecing methods.

Donna is the author of five other books: *Small Talk, Shortcuts: A Concise Guide to Rotary Cutting, A Perfect Match: A Guide to Precise Machine Piecing, Shortcuts to the Top*, and *Stripples. Shortcuts* was written for both American and metric quilters and has been translated into several languages.

The Thomas family consists of Donna, her husband, Terry, and their two teenage sons, Joseph and Peter. Terry's military career took the family many places, giving Donna the opportunity to teach all over the country as well as overseas. Terry's recent move to civilian life has given Donna visions of staying put in Pennsylvania, where she hopes to continue quilting, writing, and teaching as well as to pursue her other passion in life, gardening.